PRAISE FOR
Superhero of Love

"Heartbroken? Drowning in a sea of sadness, rage, fear, or anxiety? Whether you are the 'dumper' or the 'dumpee,' breakups are devastating. This book is a life raft as you discover how to recover, heal, and move into the life of your dreams."

—**Arielle Ford,** bestselling author of *The Soulmate Secret*

"A fabulous step-by-step guide for healing a broken heart. Bridget digs deep and teaches us how to tap into our inner wisdom and resilience to not only recover but also to make everything—including love—better than ever."

—**Nina Lorez Collins,** author of
What Would Virginia Woolf Do? And Other Questions
I Ask Myself as I Attempt to Age Without Apology

"In *Superhero of Love*, Bridget shares her transformation with honesty and guides us to our own with a bodhisattva's insight. With an angel's compassion, she never lets us down or allows us to let ourselves down."

—**Franz Metcalf, PhD,** author of *What Would Buddha Do?*
101 Answers to Life's Daily Dilemmas

"In *Superhero of Love* Bridget Fonger's writing is personal, clear, and moving. She illuminates the power of shadow work to clarify unconscious reactions and hurts to liberate true creativity and life fulfillment."

—**James Redfield,** author of *The Celestine Prophecy*

"If you feel broken and can't seem to heal, the amazing Bridget Fonger has arrived to show you that living and loving again is not only possible but inevitable if you integrate her 'Five Superpowers' into your life. Give this formula a try. Your happiness is waiting."

—**Debra Poneman,** author and founder of
Yes to Success Seminars

"Love is the greatest superpower of all. Bridget's book gives you tools to move through the pain that comes from a love lost to claim this superpower as your own."

—**Ed Bacon,** author of *8 Habits of Love:
Overcome Fear and Transform Your Life*

"This generous book offers simple, beautiful information and solutions for the ways we sabotage ourselves and subsume the negativity of those around us into our own hearts. If you're into self-help books, it's a no-brainer. If, like me, not so much, I'm telling you—okay, strongly encouraging you—to read it anyway. It will be dog-eared on my nightstand and referred to frequently for years to come. Viva Bridget Fonger, a true Superhero of Love."

—**Shanna Mahin,** author of *Oh! You Pretty Things: A Novel*

"To get past heartbreak, we first need to examine how we've dealt with the way our relationships have ended. In *Superhero of Love*, Bridget presents a breakup as a portal that has the power to propel us toward healing and a new and better future."

—**Nancy Levin,** bestselling author of
The New Relationship Blueprint
and *Jump . . . And Your Life Will Appear*

SUPERHERO
OF LOVE

HEAL YOUR BROKEN HEART
& THEN GO SAVE THE WORLD

BRIDGET FONGER

Conari Press

This edition first published in 2019 by Conari Press, an imprint of
Red Wheel/Weiser, LLC
With offices at:
65 Parker Street, Suite 7
Newburyport, MA 01950
www.redwheelweiser.com

ISBN: 978-1-57324-741-2

Library of Congress Cataloging-in-Publication Data

Names: Fonger, Bridget, 1962- author.
Title: Superhero of love : heal your broken heart & then go save the world /
  Bridget Fonger.
Description: Newburyport, MA : Conari Press, 2019.
Identifiers: LCCN 2018033904 | ISBN 9781573247412 (paperback)
Subjects: LCSH: Self-actualization (Psychology) | Divorce—Psychological
  aspects. | Love. | Happiness. | BISAC: FAMILY & RELATIONSHIPS
  / Love & Romance. | FAMILY & RELATIONSHIPS / Divorce &
  Separation. | SELF-HELP / Personal Growth / Happiness. | FAMILY &
  RELATIONSHIPS / Marriage.
Classification: LCC BF637.S4 F636 2019 | DDC 158.1—dc23
LC record available at https://lccn.loc.gov/2018033904

Cover design by T. Chick McClure and Kathryn Sky-Peck
Cover image by Bridget Fonger
Interior by Timm Bryson, em em design, LLC
Typeset in Adobe Garamond Pro

Printed in Canada
MAR

10 9 8 7 6 5 4 3 2 1

*For my father, Max, my superhero, who was driven
to awaken the Superhero of Love in me.
He teaches me still.*

Contents

Here I go
from the raging fire of
love lost
to the sweet warm nectar of
love found.
Flames no longer
out of control
singeing all they meet.
Holding
and held by
the mightiest flame of all,
the source of
all love.

Introduction: Welcome, Superhero!

What was said to the rose that made it open
Was said to me here in my chest.

Rumi

Is your heart aching from a love you lost—recently or long ago? Do you wish you could stop sabotaging yourself when it comes to love? Do you sometimes think: "This is as good as it gets?" Do you avoid opportunities to give or receive love? Do you ever wish for more love in your life—of all kinds?

If you answered yes to any of these questions, you are not alone. The good news is that you are about to discover the Superhero of Love that has always been inside you, one who can help you to give and receive love with abandon.

That Superhero has been awaiting you with wild anticipation. She knows you better than anyone, has your highest good at heart, and is yearning to help you heal and be your most powerful, loving self. There is nothing conditional about her love. It is divine love. And it is inside you right now.

I first learned of loss, and of the importance of healing from it, when I lost my father—first through divorce and then through death. Later, I discovered my own Superhero of Love while recovering from a painful romantic breakup that left me feeling like a burned up pile of ash. This book is intended as a resource, not only for those whose hearts have been broken by the loss of a romantic partner, but also for those who have suffered life-altering loss in other ways.

By the grace of God, a divine breeze blew into my own heart and stirred the ashes left behind by my loss. It cleared my heart and eyes just long enough to reveal a magnificent vision of the Superhero of Love inside me. She looked at me with gentle, knowing eyes; her gaze went straight to my heart and saw the pain I was feeling. Just as she could see inside my heart, I could see inside hers—powerful yet vulnerable, courageous, open, soft, and eager to give and receive love.

I took a good look at her. She was the vision of who I wanted to be. And I knew at that moment that I *could* be her. I didn't know exactly what I was recognizing in her, but I was inspired to begin my healing journey.

On my path, I discovered, one by one, the gifts of every Superhero of Love:

- The Mighty Flame burns inside her heart, the very source of her power. It lights her up and lights up the world around her. It guides her through life and reminds her of her connection to her own divinity, the purest essence from which her love is born.

- The five superpowers—sight, hearing, humility, self-love, and alignment—fuel her Mighty Flame and help her to love and be loved with abandon.
- She is Love Strong. She leads with her heart. Her love is her strength and it reaches out and touches others. She makes a difference in the world.

In these pages, you will embark on a journey to heal your loving heart. It's a process. You won't go from a weakling who can barely lift her own heart to flying high overnight. There isn't a magic pill or an instant cure to facilitate the change. My intention is simply that you will actually like the process of this discovery. You will read about the steps I took on my own healing journey and try them for yourself, incorporating what works into your life. My one request is that you give everything a try, even if just once. Try to keep an open mind and heart. Sometimes the best solutions come from a place you least expect, and the things we pull away from are often the very things we need to explore.

First we will awaken the Superhero of Love inside you, so that together you can discover where you have both been all your life! We will look at two elements of fire that we all deal with when facing heartache: crazy firestorms and the Mighty Flame. You will see how learning to quell the storms and fan the flame will make you Love Strong. Then we'll take a good look at two things that threaten to thwart you, both of which will end up being enormous sources of power: saboteurs and kryptonite.

You will set up your own superhero training camp with teachers and coaches, then you will assemble a support system—your Love League—made up of those who will walk alongside you on this journey. And you will work with the five superpowers of sight, hearing, humility, self-love, and alignment to bring that heart of yours into the world for boundless giving and receiving. You'll gain wisdom and learn strength-building practices that you can return to at any time.

Along the way, you will start to get some respite and, eventually, permanent relief from the pain you may be experiencing. There will be check-ins for this exact purpose, because sometimes we can't see our own transformation. This kind of reflection is both encouraging and motivating. It may even inspire you to dig a little deeper.

I give you many suggestions throughout the book that can help you on this path—like this one for entering into the world of your Superhero of Love ancestors:

Imagine you are standing amid rolling green hills; a majestic mountain range graces the distant skies, which are punctuated with fluffy clouds. Take in the beauty and grandeur of this vista. You wonder how it is that you are so blessed to be in such a wondrous place.

An ancient, holy temple rests atop one of the grassy hills, its elegant frame and pillars carved entirely of white marble.

It is luminous in the sun's light, warm and inviting. The temple is encircled by rows of smooth marble benches. You choose one and sit down; the seat is so soft it cradles you. Birds chirp softly. The sun shines on your face.

You are the only person here, yet you are not alone. You feel the comforting presence of the crowds of superheroes who have come to this place before you to gain wisdom. Centuries of holy work, divine teachings, and trainings have transpired here. You immediately feel yourself a part of this history, as if you have sat on these marble benches thousands of times.

This is the Temple of the Mighty Heart. You climb the stairs and notice the words *Ex Amor Fortitudo* etched into the arch above your head. It means "Strength through Love." At the very center of the temple, a pedestal holds a marble sculpture of an open heart that has been gently worn by the hands of a multitude of seekers paying homage. At its center, a magnificent golden torch burns with an eternal flame. The Mighty Flame burning inside you responds in recognition. You place your hand on the heart and hear a gentle voice:

Welcome to this holy mission. You have taken the first step. You are here. Now. We know about that heart of yours. First, we need you to know that we see the Superhero of Love inside you. We know your capacity for love and pain. We know your capacity to heal. We'll help you mend that heart of yours; we'll help you learn to fly. We see you. We know your greatness. We are with you, helping you hold your mighty heart.

My prayer is that you hear this call of the heart, that you never feel alone again, and that you are inspired to begin your healing journey. My hope is that you find others who are on this path with you who will encourage you to step into your greatness—whose resounding voices will echo through you, and who will help make your Mighty Flame grow. My wish is that, by the end of this book, you will come to realize that we are all superheroes who are born to fly.

Note to You, Superhero

Superheroes come in all shapes, sizes, and sexes. After all, heartaches have no gender or weight bias. So whatever your gender or sexual orientation, please translate anything you consider a "heterosexual chick" reference in this book into whatever works for you. I didn't attempt to accommodate everyone when I spoke about my ex-boyfriend by changing every "he" to "he/she/they," or by changing the word "men" to "men/women/they." Instead, I invite you to translate for yourself if "straight woman" is not your native language.

Also make your own adjustments to my references to God, Spirit, or the Divine. This book is meant to be accessible and meaningful for everyone: atheist, agnostic, Muslim, Buddhist, Catholic, or whatever faith or creed you may carry in your heart. Here you will find references to many different schools of thought, and I don't want any of them to be a barrier that prevents you from getting all you can out of this book. Whatever you consider to be a guiding force in your life is perfect.

At one point in my life, the word "God" made me bristle. Now, I think of love as my access point to God. But please don't let my references to God cause you to retreat from the basic tenets of this book. My hope and my intent are that the message is accessible and meaningful to everyone. If something I say bugs you, try to let it roll off your heart in a gentle way. I offer you the following word to say in response to anything you may find here that falls outside your own set of beliefs: *Swaha*, which is a Sanskrit word that means "so be it."

When tending sacred fires in India, Brahmin priests sing mantras as they make offerings of rice, ghee, and flowers. At the end of each mantra, they intone "Swahaaaa!" as the offering is dramatically, lovingly thrown into the sacred fire. This moves me every time I hear it, because it feels as if they are saying: "Dear sacred fire, I release this to you with love!" So, please throw whatever doesn't work for you in this book into the sacred fire.

Chapter 1

WAKE UP YOUR SUPERHERO

*A hero is someone who has given his or her life
to something bigger than oneself.*
Joseph Campbell, *The Hero's Journey*

It was my first betrayal. As soon as I discovered the intricate web of lies he had spun over the course of two years, I broke it off with the man I will refer to here as Mr. X. This breakup brought me to my knees. I thought I knew better. I thought I *was* better—better at being me, at relationships, at being aware. After many years of diligently working on myself—alone and in partnership, in and out of long-term relationships—this dramatic ending left me stunned. I thought I had done it all. I was a personal-growth ninja, for God's sake, starting in young adulthood with meditation, then individual and group therapies, then off to an ever-burgeoning and juicy spiritual practice, followed by intense personal-growth workshops, more meditation, more spiritual work, more deep dives at every opportunity. What, oh what, had I missed that had left me in this state?

Most of us have been burned at some point in our lives, left in a pile of ash by some life-altering loss. Somehow, just as in a cartoon, the little bits of nearly weightless ash, helped by a gentle breeze, become more weighted and gather into a semblance of human form again. And we carry on.

Is my head on straight? Can I put weight on both legs? Do I look human from the back, too?

Several days after I broke it off with Mr. X, I ventured out of the house with my not-so-fully formed self, acting as if I were back to normal. But I wasn't. I was walking in Old Pasadena, a rather sparkly shopping area in Southern California, hoping that the tiniest bit of its shine would rub off on me. I felt dull, gray, hunched over physically and mentally. I looked across the street at a couple who caught my eye. At that moment, the man spontaneously grabbed the woman's face between his two hands and kissed her. Mr. X used to do this—kiss me with wild abandon in public—and I loved it. He once twirled me around and dipped me dramatically in a grand hallway in Vegas and asked me to marry him. I love grand romantic gestures and, normally, witnessing any couple's private moment of bliss from across a busy street would have made me smile.

But it didn't. Instead I thought: "I wonder what lies he's telling her."

That bit of inner dialogue was my wake-up call. I knew that if I didn't start working on the internal filters creating this jaded worldview, I would never be able to open my heart fully again.

But how could I heal? I felt as if my heart and mind were on fire with incessant negative chatter: "What about *that* time?" "How about *that* woman?" "Where was he *that* night, *that* day, *that* afternoon?" "Did he mean it when he said *that?*" My thoughts were consumed with the betrayal, the many lies, as if pointing my finger at any one detail would take away the pain. But something inside me remembered that wise old saying: "When you point a finger, there are three fingers pointing back at you."

That first step I took—recognizing my own role in this state of affairs—required an inner strength that came from the yet-unrecognized Superhero of Love inside me. I forced my pointing finger back so that it pointed in the right direction—toward me. I had work to do. Me. My work. It had nothing to do with him. So, I got to work. I reached out for support and I made a commitment to be open to whatever came my way that could help me on the path to healing.

You may not believe this, but there are people all around you right now who want to help you. People really do have a natural instinct to help one another. You may not have recognized it before, but I encourage you to look at those around you with fresh eyes and to seek out people who can help you on this journey. It's simple. All you have to do is ask. Who wouldn't want to step into that beautiful Temple of the Mighty Heart with you?

Debbie Ford, who passed away in 2013, was the first coach to step into my temple. Debbie was an author and thought leader whose books continue to bring shadow work to the masses. Debbie brought all things "shadow" into the light and was as courageous and fierce as she was open-hearted. She inspired me to work with my own shadows in a way that still empowers me.

Soon my personal temple began to fill with other wise teachers. I discovered Mark Nepo's *The Book of Awakening,* which put a salve on my heart. Then came Marianne Williamson's *Enchanted Love Workshop,* which allowed me to soften and open my heart more than ever before.

Then, to conquer more of the subconscious debris inside and open myself even more to the Divine and to love, I started studying with Master John Douglas. Master John is a spiritual leader from Australia who is in the business of clearing away all that stops us from being our mightiest selves, lending divine intervention to help us remove our subconscious blocks.

These were the first superhero voices to echo in my Temple of the Mighty Heart, and they remain with me today.

You have been blessed with superheroes in your life as well. You may have just thought of some as I mentioned mine. You will gather even more around you as you progress through this book. And now you have a place to keep their wisdom thriving, a place where other wise voices can join you on your journey, a place to practice and hone your powers—your very own Temple of the Mighty Heart.

From that temple, we will begin the work of uncovering what is creating the crazy firestorms of pain that can happen after a loss. We will look at what can block your powers—saboteurs and kryptonite. And you will become very savvy about what makes the all-important Mighty Flame burn bright within you. Once you start to see what you are looking for in yourself—both what is empowering and what is disempowering—you will jump into superhero training camp to get your heart into shape, set up your Love League, and find your superhero training coaches. You will then explore the five superpowers and learn how to sharpen, test, and refine them. Finally, you will complete your pre-flight prep so you can go out into the world and spread your love far and wide!

You will hear stories that show you what it takes to be a Superhero of Love. You will complete exercises to help you increase your awareness and hone your powers. And you will get three diagnostic checks—one at the beginning, one in the middle, and one at the end of the book—that will help you chart the progress of your Mighty Flame's growth. It's important to acknowledge where you stand as you move along on your journey and, most especially, to witness your own transformation. This allows you to acknowledge how far you have come and how close you may be to unleashing your love into the world.

The more conscious you are of the Superhero of Love who has been inside you all along, the more you can attend to nurturing the Mighty Flame that is the source of her powers. In case you feel that your flame could use some extra support as you go, I have given you additional exercises at the end of the book called Mighty Flame Boosters to help fan the flame.

First, let's get a glimpse of the five superpowers that you will develop throughout the book to methodically feed your Mighty Flame. Every one of us has all five, but some are more naturally developed in each of us. You will learn to recognize and appreciate these superpowers in yourself and others. I give them here in the order in which I discovered them, as they each dive a little deeper into the heart.

SUPER SIGHT

One of your main tasks in this book is to shed some light on the unhealed corners of your heart. Super Sight helps you to look bravely at the previously unseen wounds that are keeping you stuck in your pain and anger. It allows you to remove the blinders you have put on to shield you from the truth.

If you find yourself complaining that you are always blindsided in relationships or that you keep repeating the same patterns even when you know they aren't in your best interest (or even go in the *opposite* direction of your goals), then strengthening this superpower will help you. I had to develop Super Sight to see why, even though I felt like a strong woman with high self-esteem, I found Mr. X's love far shinier and brighter than my love for myself. I had to root around in those dark corners of my heart to revisit losses I had previously experienced and shine some light on them as well. I had to have Super Sight to see what needed to be cleared away in order to uncover why I was drawn to Mr. X, and I had to rediscover the sparkle that he saw in me. I had to see it for myself to believe it and own it.

SUPER HEARING

Super Hearing allows you to hear your inner voice and follow its direction in spite of negative, disempowering chatter. You can regularly hear guidance from God, Spirit, your inner knowing, nature, or whatever higher power you acknowledge. This is the one voice that you can always trust—the one that will lead you to your highest heights. Being able to hear it clearly is a priceless gift worth pursuing.

If friends complain that you don't listen, if you have your own inner monologue that distracts you, or if you are always going nonstop, then honing this superpower will help you quiet the noise and recognize clear guidance. It helped me hear the call of love so I could move toward opportunities to love and be loved, and be of greater service to others.

SUPER HUMILITY

When you have Super Humility, you are more able to express gratitude for and acknowledge the perfect way that the Divine works through you in your life. You see as much perfection in the moments that look and feel challenging as you do in those that seem flawless. You can acknowledge the extraordinary forces that are greater than you and allow them to strengthen and open your heart even more.

If you find yourself complaining often or wallowing in self-pity, if you think that you have to do everything alone or are easily frustrated or angered by life, then cultivating humility will change your perspective. I developed my own mantra while working on this superpower: Everything is perfect just the way it is and just the way it is not. When I am swinging through the jungle of crazy emotions, I grab onto this mantra like a sturdy vine to bring me to safe, firm ground.

SUPER SELF-LOVE

Super Self-Love will help you prioritize your heart's recovery, strength, and vitality. Through it, you will be able to tap into feeling supremely loved no matter who is around you or what the circumstances may be.

If you have a pattern of saying disparaging things about yourself, if you bow out of the game of life or habitually deflect compliments, words of appreciation, or love, then you likely need to develop this superpower. And if you feel incomplete without a partner, this power is especially important to develop.

Practicing self-love helped me feel more comfortable in my skin than ever before, to know that I am just as powerful when single as I am in relationship. It taught me that the source of all love is right inside me. It always has been and always will be.

SUPER ALIGNMENT

Super Alignment allows you to tap into your highest truth at lightning speed and transcend that which stands between you and your inner knowing. You become your own divining rod, aligned with your spirit's center at every juncture.

If you think of yourself as someone who is in control, always knowing what is right and wrong—if you can be thrown off your game easily or if you push away opportunities or requests to be vulnerable—this power will serve you well. This superpower allowed me to turn inward and ask the questions that can bring me most expediently to my highest purpose and my divinity—questions like "What is my truth right now?" or "How can I best serve my soul's purpose?" And I always receive a clear answer.

CULTIVATING YOUR SUPERPOWERS

The five superpowers work together to make the Mighty Flame grow. Focusing on one power at a time can be effective, because each power reinforces the next, and each effort feeds the Superhero of Love. When you are feeling out of sorts, let yourself be guided gently toward the power that calls to you. As you do the work to develop all five powers, new traits and opportunities will reveal themselves along the way:

- An availability to love more deeply and vulnerably
- The desire to veer away from fear, anger, resignation, and apathy, and move toward love
- More time to give love to your friends, family, pets, or even strangers
- Far less negative chatter
- Courage to look at your shadows and dive deep for the gems
- The ability to dip into your inner knowing at a moment's notice
- An abundance of synchronicities and moments that make you say: "That just gave me goose bumps!"
- The absolute knowing that you are loved exactly as you are and exactly as you are not.

And in case you just went through this list with some level of impatience, cynicism, or distrust—believe me, I have *been* you—I'm going to repeat the last one: You are loved exactly as you are and exactly as you are not. Take a sip of that magic elixir. Let it seep into your heart. That superhero dose of love is just one of many you will receive on this journey.

This book will give you many tools to unveil the Superhero of Love inside you. If you can muster up some courage, open your heart a wee bit, and do the exercises, by the end of the book you will be Love Strong—able to love and be loved more than ever before.

Your love has the potential to make a huge difference in your life and in the world. Every person whose heart we spark with our hearts has the ability to spark another. Imagine a world of superhero hearts. Imagine a world of hearts whose pain no longer informs their words and actions, where saboteurs are tamed and Mighty Flames burn bright. Imagine a world full of Superheroes of Love.

Your Love Strong mission starts now. All it takes is a willingness to tap into your very own superpowers. Trust me, if *I've* got them, *you've* got them! You will be shocked at how easy it is to uncover them.

Let's begin.

Chapter 2

ORIGIN STORY

Before fixing what you're looking at,
check what you're looking through.
  Mark Nepo, *The Book of Awakening*

All superheroes have an origin story—the legend of how
they came to be and how they ended up with their superpowers. Spider-Man had his radioactive spider bite.
Wonder Woman had the Greek gods. I had my Mr. X.

We met online. I was feeling pretty good about myself
at the time. I felt as if I were a great catch who had a lot to
offer in a relationship. I was blessed with a full and happy
life—friends, travel, and work I loved. I had been single
for a few years and had worked a lot on myself during
that time, stretching my heart and mind as best I could,

increasing my integrity so I knew myself to be my word. I had just started taking tap-dancing lessons as a fun way to get out of my physical comfort zone. So, yes, I was even trying to expand the scope of my body's limits. I was excited to get back to learning the lessons that only intimate relationships can teach.

Mr. X looked happy in his profile picture and his description seemed to indicate that he had as full and happy a life as I did. That's exactly what I was looking for—a happy man who felt and knew his own power. His profile said he was in the movie industry. I assumed he was a producer, because that's what I inferred from his photo. He was filming a movie in an exotic, tropical locale when we first spoke on the phone. When it turned out that he was an actor, I winced a little, but I was already smitten by his deep voice. We connected with ease and talked for hours—him enjoying delicious rum drinks and fresh-caught grilled fish; me lying in bed at home, a dog on either side, wondering if they would like him. That, of course, would be the ultimate test.

One of the first nights we spoke on the phone, we had a very intimate conversation. A hurricane was about to hit the island where he was filming and he was seeking a little comfort, not being well-versed in the art of hurricane survival. The storm hit while we were on the phone and I thought it was adorable that he admitted he was scared; I was happy to keep him distracted. I could hear the rain pelting his windows and shutters. He made me laugh. His deep, sexy voice, which revealed a touch of vulnerability, made him instantly attractive to me. I was hooked. The next day, I left on a business trip of my own, so we continued our intimate pillow talk in late-night calls. By the time we were both back in Los Angeles, I couldn't bear to wait a moment longer to see him.

When we finally met, I realized I had become enamored with the picture of Mr. X that I had drawn in my mind. In reality, he was two inches shorter than he claimed he was in his profile, and simply wasn't what I expected based on everything revealed online or in our conversations. It wasn't that the photo was old or doctored; it just didn't portray the person who showed up on the date. Headshots capture our most spectacular selves—like catching fireflies in a jar. When I met him in person, I thought: "Oh, he's not my guy." We had a nice talk, though, and I thought he could be a friend. Then, just minutes before the date was to end, he touched the back of my hand very gently with one finger as he made a point. I have no idea what the point was, but I remember how he smiled and playfully tilted his head as his touch sent energy thrilling through my body. Whatever words he uttered, I heard: "You're mine." And my inner voice responded: "Yes. That voice, that humor, that touch. I'm yours." So, I let myself fall.

I enjoyed the fall. We had fun. We made each other laugh a lot. We started traveling together. He was a good traveler, even when emergencies came up. We relaxed, we enjoyed each other, and we had amazing sex. He made me feel like a woman again, after a long dry spell from dating. He appreciated me. We loved to cook together and entertain. He adored me and I adored him right back. My friends loved him because they saw how happy I was with him. And he was mighty charismatic, so they all fell a little in love with him, too.

So when I found out that he had told me a rather enormous lie, which unraveled a whole web of other lies told over the course of our years together, my dearest friends were nearly as devastated as I was. I remember wondering if a couple of them were more disappointed for themselves than for me. He was cool. I got it. But we all also knew that the extent of his lies was too great for me to continue the relationship. The pictures of what I thought the future was going to look like all crashed around me at once.

Shattered glass everywhere. Where do I step now? How do I move forward?

This devastating moment was seminal to my own origin story. Every superhero has one. You're reading mine. You have your own, and tapping into it will help you unravel the many threads of that story that brought you to this exact moment in your life.

Love Strong Exercise: Your Origin Story

Whether it happened yesterday, last week, last month, last year, or even decades ago—and no matter what kind of loss it was that led you here—it's time to get in touch with the story of your heartbreak and what it all means. Think about the loss you are experiencing. Then silently answer the following questions, or record yourself answering them on your device, or write them in a journal or on the blank pages provided at the end of this book.

- What do you want to acknowledge about the good times?
- Were there any red flags you set aside early on?
- What events can you not release? Do their memories still leave you feeling powerless, paralyzed, or just plain sad or mad?
- What words originally spoken by someone else (it doesn't matter how long ago they were uttered) do you keep replaying in your head like a bad recording?
- What have you been saying to yourself since this loss—about your life, about your state of mind, about your value?
- What dream of your future did you abandon (accidentally or on purpose) because of this loss?
- If you could stand on the edge of the Grand Canyon and scream, with no danger of being heard, what would you release into that abyss about this loss?
- Is there anything else that you need to say about yourself or your life right now to give a good picture of how you feel, think, or see the world?

Mighty Flame Check-In #1

Welcome to your first Mighty Flame Check-In—the first of three that you will find throughout this book. These check-ins will allow you to see how the book is working for you and help you track your progress as you grow more Love Strong. They don't take very long to do and it can be fun to track how your Mighty Flame grows!

We will dive more deeply into what fans or dims your Mighty Flame in coming chapters. In this first check-in, we will simply take a reading of the state of your heart at the beginning of your journey. Rate your answers on a scale of 0 to 10—or 10 to 0. The goal is to have all your responses move to the right side of the scale as you progress.

My heart pain level is about:

10　9　8　7　6　5　4　3　2　1　0

My energy level is about:

0　1　2　3　4　5　6　7　8　9　10

My obsessive thinking about my loss is roughly:

10　9　8　7　6　5　4　3　2　1　0

My joy quotient is about:

0　1　2　3　4　5　6　7　8　9　10

Chapter 3

FROM CRAZY FIRESTORMS TO THE MIGHTY FLAME

Last year, I gazed at the fire,
This year I'm burnt kabob.
Thirst drove me down to the water
Where I drank the moon's reflection.

—Rumi

I felt very much like a burnt kabob when I first unraveled the Mr. X betrayals. Even if your breakup didn't leave you burned to a crisp, it's impossible not to be singed when you experience loss, with little pieces of your heart set ablaze. As a Superhero of Love, you must take a two-pronged approach to these fires: first soothe and cool the crazy firestorms, then feed the Mighty Flame that powers you. This chapter will show you the difference between these two sources of fire, because one will take you down, while the other will build you up.

Crazy firestorms are those times when we feel out of control, angry and on edge, or caught in repetitive negative thinking. These firestorms can be adrenaline-pumping yet energy-depleting wild fires that wreak havoc and destruction on our hearts and minds. They can burn so deep and wide that they lead to depression, unshakable sadness, apathy, or self-loathing. And they can start and spread without you even noticing.

The Mighty Flame, however, is peaceful, easily focused, and gently warming to the soul. It is where joy and contentment reside. When your Mighty Flame burns bright, you can be vulnerable and powerful at the same time because you know your guiding light is love. You can be present, in your skin. You feel ease, not dis-ease or discomfort, with what is so. You experience the gentle flow of love in and out—no matter what the circumstance.

Crazy firestorms and the Mighty Flame are opposites, yet they both require the same vigilant attention. Firestorms spark repetitive negative thoughts, frenetic energy, confusion, hopelessness, mental chatter, reaching outward, and anger that won't quit. The Mighty Flame, on the other hand, encourages peaceful centeredness, calm, clarity, hope, mental quietude, reaching inward, and joy.

CRAZY FIRESTORMS

When I was in the middle of the crazy firestorms that followed my breakup with Mr. X, I couldn't imagine relief ever coming. Many of my girlfriends experience insomnia when they're in the throes of these firestorms. I don't. But, while I could sleep through the night, I often woke up exhausted from working so hard in my dreams. My days felt like crazy mountain-climbing expeditions in which I first trudged uphill against the sadness, then ran back down into the valleys aflame with anger. Up and down, up and down, always running away from some uncomfortable emotion.

One evening, I went out with my (at the time) ninety-six-year-old friend, Adelaide, for a little respite. Adelaide is my dear friend Beanie's grandma who has been a source of Love League wisdom since I was eleven. She loves to give advice regarding relationships. She earned it: married over sixty years until the death of her husband. The first tidbit she gave me, when I was in a long-term relationship in my twenties, was always to have my own secrets. I still want to try out that one. Sounds juicy.

Adelaide loved Mr. X, so she was upset about the breakup. I saw her right after it happened and told her that I couldn't imagine ever falling in love again. She responded: "Well, of course not; you've been singed." She was right. It was then that I realized how those little singes can re-ignite old firestorms from the past. In fact, a recent loss can ignite a full-blown inferno if you haven't healed the wounds of your past. One of Adelaide's greatest gifts to me is being a grounding force in the face of my drama-queen perspectives. The loss of Mr. X was a singe, not an inferno. And it was my job to manage what I had let grow into a crazy firestorm.

In the days after the breakup with Mr. X, I knew I had to deal with my pattern of seeking power outside of myself. Even though I felt confident and mighty kick-ass when I was not in a relationship, as soon as I got into one, my sense of self-worth became dependent upon my partner. I used the love from my partner to light up my heart, rather than relying on my own Mighty Flame, which was patiently waiting to be discovered. But when you are engulfed in a firestorm, it's easy to lose sight of that flame.

What flame? What fire? All I know is it's hot in here, and not the good kind of hot.

When one of my friends was ghosted by a man she had been dating, she found herself deep in the frenzy of a firestorm, trying to figure out what had gone wrong. Why had he suddenly cut off all contact with her? What had she done to cause his sudden flight? She couldn't have a conversation about anything else, and wanted everyone to help her figure out this conundrum. How? Why? When? What?

None of us had any interest in figuring it out. We just wanted her to realize that she had dodged a bullet. Who wants to be in a relationship with someone who would do this to a potential mate? From the outside looking in, it was a blessing. From the inside looking out—well, there were a lot of flames obscuring her view.

I was no different at the beginning of my journey. After my breakup with Mr. X, firestorms plagued me with two kinds of negative feelings: one directed outside—anger—and one directed inside—sadness. The angry thoughts were easy to understand. I knew *when* I was mad and I knew *why* I was mad. For a while, the anger even made me feel righteous and empowered, as if I were better than Mr. X.

Some anger can be genuinely helpful. It can give us the gumption we need to take action that might otherwise be impossible to take. I know women who had to experience dramatic infidelities before deciding to end their marriages. One friend found out that her husband was not only cheating on her, but had taken their toddler on his escapades. Imagine her fury and the fire that catapulted her from this marriage.

In many cases, the anger builds over the course of the relationship and is not fully managed through all its incarnations. But righteous anger can spur a righteous move. Sometimes God has to hit us over the head with a frying pan! We can almost be grateful for the theatrical end, because we might not have left otherwise.

I didn't really get angry until after the breakup with Mr. X, when it all came crashing down in an avalanche of lies. Several weeks after the breakup, a few different people came forward with confessions of what they had known.

I discovered that the lying was even more pervasive than I had thought. This hit me on a new level.

What? More lies? Impossible! I can't even . . .

And then, the mother of all lies: He. Was. Married.

Married. The many times he used the words "divorced" and "ex-wife" were merely shiny distractions to keep me moving forward. To be fair, his wife had had a boyfriend long before we met, and he had had at least a couple of relationships before ours. But the blood drained from my body when I heard the two syllables: mar-ried. They seemed to drip out of our mutual friend's mouth in slow motion. I repeated the word out loud to confirm, tagging on the most enormous question mark so she knew to take extra care in her response.

"I assumed you knew," was her reply.

I didn't know. And I hadn't spoken to him since our parting. I had only heard that he had become involved with someone new immediately after the breakup, and thought I might hear of a quick marriage to that person but never expected this about the woman I knew as his ex-wife. Needless to say, I had a very dramatic reaction to this news. Sometimes some serious acting out is warranted. I think I spent several days on the phone. I needed everyone to know. Every. One. If I could have, I would have hired a skywriter.

After my dramatic, days-long performance, I was ready to get back to superhero business, to take a deep dive and come to understand that the situation was really nothing more than Mr. X being Mr. X and me being me, each protecting ourselves. He wasn't brave enough to tell the truth, and I wasn't brave enough to hear the truth. I had to forgive us both—myself for putting on the blinders and him for lying.

Days after learning he was still married, I had dinner with a friend who owns the best little dress shop in Old Pasadena. She hesitantly told me that Mr. X had recently been in the store with his new girlfriend. While she was in the dressing room, he had asked if his girlfriend could use my discount. To add further insult to injury, he had whispered to the salesperson, so his girlfriend couldn't hear, that *he* had broken up with *me* because I couldn't get along with his daughter. I hit the roof! That lie was somehow even more egregious than all the others, if such a thing were possible.

The lid that I had been struggling with all my might to keep on the pot flew off. I kept myself together at dinner, but only because I was in shock. My girlfriend and her husband did their darnedest to buffer the blow and soothe me. The next day, however, my anger seemed to take on a visible, monstrous shape and send slime everywhere. Slime all over my house. Slime on the phone lines leading to all my girlfriends. I called one girlfriend, spewed ugly thoughts and feelings, then hung up, my heart barely relieved. Soon after, I needed to call someone else. Each time I hung up, I was embarrassed that I had tainted yet another friendship with all this anger. But I couldn't let it go. Anger had taken the wheel and was driving the car of my life. It had summarily thrown me into the back seat. I realized that the first thing I needed to do to regain control of the car was to have my anger heard—not by yet another girlfriend, but by Mr. X.

I wrote a letter. Not an email or a text. An honest-to-god letter that I put in an envelope with a stamp on it. I asked him to stop lying about me, about how and why we had broken up. And I told him that his friends had admitted other lies they knew of, and that I was more informed than he might think. I let go of all that I was struggling to keep inside.

The act of writing a letter like this can make you feel like a wizard. When I wrote it, the anger transmuted to acceptance—not apathy, but acceptance of what was so. Things happened between us. I was angry and I needed to communicate that anger honestly and completely. Each step—writing, addressing the envelope, sealing it, putting the stamp on it, and dropping it in the mailbox—caused little shifts in my heart. My feelings were given a voice. You may not even need to send the letter, you may just need to hear your own deep and powerful lion's roar. In my case, I wanted to stop any further lies, so I sent it. I wasn't the only one who needed to hear my roar.

Then I got to work on me. I had to untangle what had really happened from the dramatic story I had made up. What were the facts?

- He told lies.
- I wasn't a victim.
- He was being him, and I was being me.

- We chose each other and we were still playing our parts perfectly.
- I could forgive us both—again.

Several days later, he replied to my letter with a long letter of his own, but only these four lovely words mattered: "Your anger is justified." I still find that response to be just about as miraculous as they come. As a result, forgiveness was his, and peace was mine.

If you don't receive justification from your Mr. X, find a dear friend who will acknowledge your anger or your pain for you. You can role play with friends, telling them exactly what you need them to say to you. You can even write it down for them like a script and have them say it to you exactly as you need to hear it. Tell them what you need them to hear and then have them repeat their lines as many times as necessary.

Acknowledgment is a powerful tool, because it grounds us in the present moment, and it can calm the crazy firestorms. Face it: when you are in a firestorm, you are pretty much entrenched in the past. I was so entrenched in looking at Mr. X's misdeeds that I was nearly buried alive. His acknowledgment gave me the shovel I needed to dig myself out of my obsession with the past.

Let's move our way back into the present moment now, sweetheart. Right this way . . .

Acknowledgment not only quells your crazy firestorms, it also nurtures your Mighty Flame. I had a friend who was very angry about having cancer. I took her to her favorite beach, which had a private cove. For the good part of an afternoon, she yelled and screamed and let all that anger out. My job was just to bear witness and to provide her with an endless supply of rocks to throw at the cliff. Did the anger at her cancer end that day? Not at all. But the acknowledgment of it lit up her Mighty Flame. By the end of the day, she was glowing. The experience gave her relief from the grief and a place to return to in her heart when the anger rose up again.

Grief, sadness, anger, and rage can all take turns creating fires. In the very darkest days after my breakup with Mr. X, I felt knocked down by both anger and sadness. Anger exhausted me and sadness was an ever-present leaden, smoldering cloak weighing me down. I often felt as if I didn't have the strength to lift it off my shoulders. The more I fought it, the worse it got.

Sad, repetitive thoughts can be insidious and disempowering. They can ebb less frequently than anger, so the respites between them are fewer and farther apart. And before you know it, you are drowning in them. Sad thoughts are like deep, dark waters. You can't even see where the light is, so you never know where to come up for air.

Most important, if you're too busy fighting, you can't see the source of these thoughts. I always want to run through uncomfortable emotions like a freight train, as if my feelings are enemies that need to be mowed down. In reality, they are like white surrender flags saying: "Look here, please!" My friend Fran has received more than her share of calls from me with complaints that I can't stop crying or that I am "still" sad. She always patiently repeats: "Of course you're sad. And, that's okay." I don't know how many times she has repeated these words over the decades: "Be gentle with yourself." It was in the midst of my breakup with Mr. X that I finally was able to hear her.

Sometimes you just need to be sad, and sometimes you just need to be mad. But if the crazy firestorms don't quit or if they feel out of proportion to your circumstances, you may want to explore what's underneath that top layer of grief. We will learn how to do that in the next chapter. For now, you need to know that the more you ignore the source of the fire, the more you end up shutting down the parts of yourself that are begging to be remembered, nurtured, or given a voice.

Crazy firestorms are God's way of shining light on the unfinished business in your heart. Consciously dealing with that unfinished business can be thrilling, can bring you deep relief, and will always prove worth the effort.

YOUR MIGHTY FLAME

The other source of fire that is essential to your recovery is your Mighty Flame. Have you ever had the experience of "knowing" or "feeling" something to be true? A time when your intuition was spot on and you felt as if you were divinely guided? That's your Mighty Flame at work. It has been with you since the very beginning. It is what fed your first cry of life, your first smile. It gave you the urge to propel yourself forward and upward. It is what makes you reach for love.

If you take only one concept away from this book, I wish it to be this: Your Mighty Flame gives you the power to love and be loved. It gives you the power to fly as a Superhero of Love, to touch other hearts, and to make a difference in the world. And here is the best news: Although you may not feel a connection to your own Mighty Flame yet, and even if you don't believe me that it exists, I am here to promise you it is there. And, even better, although that flame may wane at times, it will never ever die.

The Mighty Flame is inside every superhero. It fuels our super-humanity, sending us beyond, farther, deeper. Like the Olympic flame, it can travel the world, igniting one torch after another, each flame born of the same fire. Such is the journey of our own hearts. We spend our days touching, inspiring, and sparking each other's hearts with our Mighty Flames, whether we know it or not.

Once I became aware of my flame and came to terms with how I had neglected it or abused its power, I realized its importance. I had ignored it. I had dropped the torch. Too often. Don't get me wrong, it's natural to drop this torch. Don't beat yourself up when you do. Just pick it back up. You'll find that flame is damned forgiving.

I first became aware of my own Mighty Flame when I was in the midst of a housing crisis. My landlord told me that I had two months to move. I embarked on the crazy, mad adventure of trying either to buy a house quickly or to find that elusive unicorn, an affordable rental house. I started by making a list of things I wanted in my new home. I created a beautiful collage and remained conscious of my vision. But, because time was so limited, I began to doubt if I would find as nice a place as I wanted in the price range I could afford.

Maybe this is as good as it gets. Maybe I can live with less.

Oh, the humanity of doubt! Luckily, before one house-viewing appointment, I had a session with my coach. She told me to be conscious of the flame inside me before I walked into the house and to keep checking in with it as I moved from room to room. I entered the house and the flame dimmed. This couldn't be my home. It was clear. Even though there was a lot that felt right about the house, and as much as I wanted it to be right, it wasn't.

When you become proficient at monitoring your Mighty Flame, it can be a huge relief. The clarity it brings is stunning. It's like being able to see perfectly after needing glasses your whole life.

Imagine applying this same intuition to love!

I did. I went on dates with some wonderful men. Just as I did with the perfectly wonderful houses, I checked in with my flame. And, just as with the houses, it was sometimes shocking when the flame dimmed.

What? He seemed so cool! I liked that, and that, and even that.

You can certainly make choices about important things in your life by using your mind alone: "That man will make a good father," or "This house is in a perfect location." But imagine your purest, unfiltered intuition leading you through life. Imagine trusting it as an unfaltering compass.

All may not instantly become crystal clear when you first test it out. I walked into the house that ended up being the perfect house for me and my flame clearly said, "Yes!" But my mind had some objections. I talked with a friend to clear the clutter out of my mind and was then able to feel my flame. It was still a yes. Even my real estate agent came to know within seconds of us entering a house if it was going to work for me. The house I chose is one I couldn't help but keep coming back to, because my flame grew every time. I was the moth to its flame, happy just to sit in front of it, staring at its light.

Days later, as I packed up the old house, I found my collage and the list of all the qualities I wanted in my new dream house. I had it all—and more! You never have to settle. Ever. When you let your inner flame, your highest self, guide you, you can't go wrong. In fact, you can have more than you ever imagined.

Be mindful of your Mighty Flame. Notice what makes it grow and what makes it dim. As you learn what it needs, you can consciously nourish it.

Over the last several years, when alone and full of bliss, with my Mighty Flame burning bright, I have found myself exclaiming aloud: "I love my life!" Yet, there have been times when I clearly felt the opposite. I once missed a plane and was struggling to find an alternate flight to get to an appointment on time. I ran through the airport harried. I wasn't in love with my life in that moment. I was covered with sweat, full of panic over the clients I might disappoint, and berating myself for not knowing that my flight was taking off from a bizarre far-off terminal due to airport construction. I couldn't have known this fact, and yet guilt was searing into my heart as I ran.

You should have known. Bad girl. Bad and wrong girl. Bad. Bad. Bad.

My life was not perfect in that moment, because I felt I was not perfect. When you repeat something to yourself, it starts to become true, right? Luckily, I recognized what was happening and got my wits about me. I stopped in the middle of an empty corridor and said aloud: "I love my life!" This, of course, made me laugh because I was a hot mess. Then I added: "I love me even when I am bad and wrong." Teasing myself for the ridiculous repeating of untruths, just as friends sometimes do, puts everything back in perspective. And laughter will always instantly fan your Mighty Flame.

THE POWER OF INTEGRITY

While I love to laugh, the number-one method I use to fan my Mighty Flame is integrity. Integrity is jet fuel for your heart. It will feed your Mighty Flame. Having integrity means:

- You are your word. You do what you say you are going to do. You are known for keeping your promises.
- You empower yourself and others with your word, your actions, and your way of being.
- People know they can count on you, no matter what.
- Your friends and loved ones know you as someone who achieves goals and dreams. And in your most exalted state, you are a person who makes dreams come true for others.
- You speak well of yourself and others.

That last one is my Achilles heel. I am most often out of integrity when I disempower myself or someone else. Reining in my negative thoughts about myself or others is a challenge when my flame is dim. Yet reining in your negative thoughts is precisely what will make that flame grow. It's a practice. Whatever you can do to remind yourself that you are practicing, that you are in the game of empowering with your words, the better off you will be.

Working on integrity can be fun, because you can make it like a game. Shoot integrity hoops: have a goal, make a goal; give your word, keep your word. Aim for minimal disempowerment and maximum empowerment.

Being out of integrity comes in many forms, but here's a list of things you may be doing that won't help your Mighty Flame:

- Speaking ill of others
- Speaking ill of yourself
- Having your environment out of order (a reflection of internal disorder)
- Being chronically late
- Not keeping promises

For many people, the end of a relationship comes the moment they let their integrity slip, when they break a promise to themselves. I know a woman who told her partner she would not move in with him until he was sober. He cleaned up his act and they moved in together. Almost immediately, his drinking resumed. Did my friend redraw the line in the sand and move out? No. That was the defining moment that led to the end of their relationship. She knew she should move out immediately, but she didn't. The relationship disintegrated.

At one point in my relationship with Mr. X, he spoke of living together. I replied that I wouldn't move in without being engaged. I made this promise to myself years before and I let him know I intended to keep the commitment. Not too long after this, I decided I was not going to spend another summer without central air conditioning, and I started looking for a new place to live. Mr. X insisted we look for houses to move into together, that it made sense since we would soon be engaged and moving in together anyway. He made it sound fun and reasonable, and I threw my promise out the window as we sped off to look at the first possible house.

The excitement wore off over the course of the day. As we parted ways that evening, I felt as if something were really not right. My Mighty Flame was so dim that it left me chilled. My actions were not reflective of the promise I made to myself. Mr. X said he was going to ask me to marry him several months down the line, when his daughter went to college. He wanted me to trust his commitment. I didn't trust either of us at that point. I had drawn a line in the sand and was stomping all over it. On some level, we both knew it was over at the end of that day. We parted ways like two deflated balloons. We couldn't pretend to hold our-selves up, let alone our love within the relationship. Even though we had technically not yet parted ways, we knew we had come to the end of the line.

When one of my friends got remarried, she and her new husband blended their two families, Brady Bunch style. As much as their therapist encouraged them to make clear agreements with each other to help guide them during their merger, they instead trusted that their love would pull them through any conflict. Many disagreements ensued as their parenting styles clashed. They weren't working as a team, and they often disempowered each other in the eyes of their children. Love helps, but integrity makes everything work better. Integrity helps love grow, giving it healthy soil and a protective fence to keep it safe, nourished, and nurtured.

I mentioned that I had the great boon of being forced to move just a few months after this breakup. Although I had been dying to move anyway, it felt like horrible timing. I was in the middle of a crazy firestorm. Then I embraced it as an opportunity for a fresh start. It was the best thing that could have happened at that moment for my Mighty Flame.

When I moved, I gave away or sold almost every stick of furniture, donated several carloads of "the past," and got rid of all that should have been gone long before. Not only did I get a much better, amazing house, but I also bought all new furniture and spread myself out in my beautiful surroundings in a way that allowed my soul to open up. I felt like a butterfly settling on a beautiful, newly bloomed flower, blissfully surrounded by more flowers, trees, and beauty than I could have dreamed.

Not everyone has the synchronistic opportunity to move after a huge breakup, but you can still work on the integrity of your home. Refresh and renew; let go and clean out. All of these actions allow your soul to breathe a little better. Clearing out the past is always life-giving and life-affirming.

Putting things in order makes your life flow and clears away obstacles—literally and figuratively. Tripping over clutter in either your physical space or in your mind keeps you from reaching your destination. Without integrity, life just doesn't work as well. In the laboratory of my life, I have evidence that this is true. When I am in integrity, the circuits are clean, and my energy and power can flow. I make things happen. My energy is lighter.

To recap, having integrity means:

- You say what you mean and mean what you say.
- You do what you say you are going to do.
- Your life (house, car, office, finances, etc.) is in order.
- You are on time, respectful of your time and the time of others.
- You are known as a person who can be counted on, who always keeps her word.

From the big things like moral character, to the small things like having a clean fridge, having integrity makes life work better.

Sometimes I think I don't have the time to stop and get things into integrity, but I know I get an extra kick in my step and a surge of energy when I do. Start noticing how being out of integrity can drag you and your flame down. With very few exceptions, even the messiest people don't feel good about sitting in the middle of chaos. It wears on you—often without you even realizing it—and it definitely inhibits your productivity. Chaos outside is a reflection of chaos inside. And chaos tends to invite even more chaos.

Buddying up in the name of integrity is always a good idea to make it feel more like a game. On any given morning, Monday through Friday, at the same time each day, you can find me on a call with two to four friends. We each declare three tasks we will do that day in three different areas of our lives we want to transform. The next morning, we report how we did—three out of three, two out of three, etc. If I don't hit three out of three, I always take responsibility for what took me out of the game so I can stay conscious of the patterns that derail my integrity.

One of the most powerful things I can do on these calls is to commit to at least fifteen minutes of getting something into integrity. I don't have to know at the time what work I will do. I let myself choose over the course of the day. There's always something that can be sifted through, reorganized, cleaned, or completed after being left half-done. Without fail, my flame gets a boost, and I always end up working on whatever I choose for far more time than I originally promised. I highly recommend having a buddy, or ideally a group of buddies, with whom you can practice this. Find people who care about making a shift in their own lives, who already have a strong relationship with their word, and who inspire you. You will become a source of inspiration in this game as well—like the Superhero of Love that you are!

When your flame is growing and your life is working with integrity like a well-oiled machine, you will start to hear the hum of your Mighty Flame. You may even be more inclined to sing spontaneously when that flame is burning bright. Anything that makes your heart and soul sing, or helps you hear your own song, is a good thing. When you are guided by your own song rather than the noisy chatter of your mind, you will see the world differently and interact with others in a new way.

The following exercise will help clear the airwaves so you can hear that beautiful song, by getting some practice with calming crazy firestorms and increasing your Mighty Flame's power.

Love Strong Exercise: From Firestorm to Flame

Think of a time when you felt out of control. Imagine you are right back in that moment and answer the following questions:

- What's the cause of this crazy firestorm?
- The three emotions I feel are: _____, _____, and _____.
- What do I need right now to get some relief?
- Is there anything I could ask of someone to help me get some relief? If yes, who is the perfect person to ask?
- Is there something I can do to shift the focus back to my Mighty Flame? When can I do it?

Make a commitment to yourself. If you don't come up with anything to do, or anyone to reach out to, no worries. Something may pop into your head later, and you can commit then to an action.

For now, take this moment to stop and give yourself as much time as you can to imagine the Mighty Flame in the center of your chest. Just breathe into that flame with awareness. You can repeat: "I bow to the Mighty Flame inside me. I bow to the Mighty Flame inside me."

Just by giving your Mighty Flame attention, you commit a super-heroic act.

Chapter 4

SABOTEURS

*You must go into the dark in order to bring
forth your light.*

Debbie Ford,
The Dark Side of the Light Chasers

We often think of superheroes in terms of the epic bat-
tles they valiantly fight with their enemies, where good
triumphs over evil, and light over dark. Batman foils the
Penguin's plan to devalue Gotham's currency; Superman
swoops in at the last minute to defeat an assassination attempt. We Superheroes of Love must look inside to meet
our mightiest foes. It's not the shadows in the dark alleys
we need to confront, but those inside us. In this chapter, I

hope to inspire you to be curious about the previously un-noticed places in your heart where your shadow selves live, and to empower you to deal with your shadows when they become saboteurs and wreak havoc in your life.

Have you ever become enraged when someone cut you off in traffic or in the grocery line? Have you lost it when someone spoke down to you or made you feel stupid? Have you ever overreacted and then later regretted it? Do you sometimes feel angry, but don't know the source of your fury?

Renowned psychiatrist and psychoanalyst Carl Jung developed the concept of our shadow selves as the pieces of ourselves we suppress, deny, or ignore that recede into our subconscious. Because we are not consciously aware of them, they can become stealthy little bombers that strike when we least expect it—for instance, when we are in line at the grocery store and become supremely annoyed by someone in front of us.

Shadows become saboteurs when they take control and hinder us or cause us pain. Shadows are constantly oper-ating, influencing, and driving our choices. The moments they tend to grab our full attention are when we label what they are doing as sabotage. And that's a good thing. When they shift into the role of saboteurs, we wake up to them. Where they may have been just background noise that we could previously tune out, they are now screaming: "Look inside; get to know me. I am not going away. I need you."

Whenever you feel less than your most powerful self—steeped in anger, easily triggered by others, paralyzed by fear, enveloped by blankets of dark sadness—you can likely benefit from doing some shadow work. You don't have to wait for your shadows to scream for your attention. Hopefully, as we continue to discuss shadows and how they become saboteurs, you will start to become more cognizant of their wily ways.

Let's say, right up front, that it's normal that we remain unconscious of our shadow selves. They are, after all, *sub*conscious, flying under the radar of our day-to-day awareness. Normally, we focus on what's in front of us, what we can access with our five senses. But we all have subconscious desires and motivations that are completely disconnected from our conscious dreams and wishes, and these have the potential to wipe out our higher aspirations. Imagine someone who wants to marry and have kids, but has a subconscious desire to remain free and untethered. This is an example of the shadow steering the car and taking us where we don't want to go. Otherwise, why would we end up where we don't want to be?

You may have fallen prey to your shadow if you:

- Do things that you know you will regret
- Feel out of sorts and don't understand why
- Say yes to things that will cause you pain
- Can't remove yourself from a source of pain

- Say you want one thing, but consistently create something altogether different
- Feel as if you are treading water

Shadows are born when bad things happen to us, or when perfectly mundane things happen to us as children. Yet, from that innocent perspective, we perceived them as traumatic events. And trauma, whether perceived or actual, has happened to all of us.

I will never forget how distressing my first day of school was. It's a normal event in any young child's life, but for some of us, it was traumatic. I couldn't understand why I had to leave my comfortable home, my toys, and my mom and go to a completely foreign place for hours on end.

Mom must not love me anymore if I have to come here now.

I don't care how idyllic your childhood was, at some point you were put in a situation that brought up complex emotions that you were not equipped to process. No matter how insignificant we judge an event from our childhood to be when seen from our present adult perspective, as children, we did not have the emotional acuity or appropriate experience to help process the pain of that moment. To an adult, the same event might not cause any pain at all, of course. But it's the feelings that we could not process as children and pushed into our subconscious that we must attend to now. Little pieces of our emotional selves may be left behind in those moments—stuck at that age, with the corresponding thoughts and feelings etched in stone. That's a shadow and a potential saboteur.

Children often require reassurance to curb their fears and questions about the world. Shadow selves are no different. In a way, shadows are children—the children we left behind who need the reassurance they should have received long ago. I know that my own shadows have risen to saboteur status when I overreact, become judgmental, or push people away. Here are some of the questions I ask myself to determine what I am doing to trigger them:

- Where have I let down my healthy boundaries?
- Where have I jumped into a relationship too deep, too fast?
- Is that little girl feeling unsafe emotionally or physically?
- Have I compromised myself for someone else?

Once I've made an inquiry, I can go back to my shadow and tell her what I am going to do to remedy the situation. Shadows love to hear that we've got their backs. I sometimes have to repeat for one: "I've got this, I've got this. I promise."

It's me and my shadow, as the song says. It's not a matter of split personalities. We all have these disenfranchised shadow selves inside of us. But you don't need to have a five-year-old, a seven-year-old, or even a thirteen-year-old at the wheel. You need to integrate your shadows into your adult superhero self and manage their needs so you can drive the car exactly where you want to go, without losing control of the wheel mid-adventure and being steered into a ditch.

Unfortunately, no one can do this work for you. It's what they call an "inside job." We must go in and introduce the unhealed, disenfranchised little ones inside us to the conscious adult who is now in charge of their safety and care. We need to hear them, give them love, and integrate them into our adult selves so we can be whole and powerful. They are appropriately named, tucked away in the *shadows,* hidden from our view. It is our job to reach into that dark closet and recognize and embrace those parts of ourselves that were never fully expressed, nurtured, and healed.

I imagine it like this: I have a little closet in my heart. I open it. It's dark inside, but one by one, my shadow selves come out of the darkness into the doorway, and the light shines upon them. As they come forward, they smile, so happy that I am recognizing them, but shy, as they are not used to the attention. One by one, they reveal themselves and gently reach toward me with a closed fist. Then they turn that fist over and open it to reveal a handful of sparkling jewels. Their smiles grow even bigger as they see me smile. In that moment, we are both known, understood, and forgiven—me for having pushed them down into the darkness and them for acting out to gain my attention.

Those shadows and the jewels they carry can appear in different ways—some as strengths we develop:

- As the "bitchy" shadow who stands up for others, makes a difference in the world, and doesn't take no for an answer.
- As the "shy" shadow who is swift to acknowledge others, is humble, and has an internal life that allows her to have compassion and empathy.
- As the "angry" shadow who makes you gifted as an artist or an activist who deeply moves people with her passions, incites change, and makes things happen with her fire.
- As the "fearful" shadow whose cautious, methodical ways bring her attention to detail to an art form.

Diving in to uncover these shadows—the little pieces of ourselves that we have forgotten, disenfranchised, or inadvertently ignored—is the cornerstone of our superhero work. I'll give you plenty of tools to work with these shadows when they rise up. But first, let's look at how they may reveal themselves in relationships.

I thought Mr. X was my nemesis. He was the evil liar. He was my Joker, my Lex Luthor. I could have rallied entire cities to agree with me and applaud my righteous anger. Fairly quickly, though, I discovered that my true nemesis was right inside me—that there were things hidden and unseen, pushed just under the surface of my consciousness, that brought me to him. I saw that he was, in fact, not evil. Neither of us were. We were both just at the mercy of our own shadows, our saboteurs. It wasn't until a few weeks after the breakup with Mr. X that I recognized one of my own shadows that had become a saboteur in the relationship.

My father separated from my mother when I was about six years old and divorced her when I was seven. I made up the story with my little-girl reasoning that my dad left because I was not perfect. In my six-year-old mind, their relationship's end had nothing to do with either my mom or my dad; it was all my fault. That little shadow self was born, and I went through life with her mantra playing in a continuous loop: I'm not good enough. Upon uncovering this belief, I realized that I had chosen Mr. X because he made me feel "good enough." I had not entered the relationship from a place of power. The little girl inside me just wanted to feel "good enough," and Mr. X made her feel that way.

Oh, well, if he likes me, then maybe I am good enough!

But soon, that little shadow started to cause trouble, because she wasn't truly empowered, nurtured, or even heard. So she turned the criticism on him: now *he* wasn't good enough.

It's a sign that we are falling prey to our shadows' shenanigans when we:

- Seek outside assurances of our power
- Are triggered by another's behavior
- Speak in ways that don't match our chronological age
- Overreact and are out of control
- Make accusations and point fingers at others

In this relationship, my saboteur pointed toward Mr. X so much that it was as if one finger were cast in cement pointing in his direction.

It's easy to see when others are sabotaging themselves, but not so easy to catch ourselves when we are slowly sinking into quicksand. Saboteurs are tricky. They have a knack for making us believe that we are on firm ground. When my saboteurs are in control, I get stubborn and self-righteous, as if I am on a battlefield fighting for my life. I feel a false sense of power, but the more I fight, the more confused and upset I feel. I need to stop, look for the part of me that is upset, grab her hand, and lead her off that field, even if she's kicking and screaming.

In the classic Humphrey Bogart movie *The Treasure of Sierra Madre,* there's a famous line uttered by a defiant Mexican in response to Bogey's request that he show his badge to prove he is a policeman. The line is remembered (slightly incorrectly) as: "We don't need no stinkin' badges!" I've heard many people declare just as defiantly that they don't have "no stinkin' shadows," and I think of that movie every time. Our shadows can give us a false sense of power, making us feel as if we've got it all together.

It can help to give names to your shadow selves to make them feel more alive and relatable. It helps you to see them as friends with whom you can chat, to whom you can listen and respond as a caring companion, confidante, or loving parent. Wendy has always felt like a light-hearted name to me, so I chose it for the first shadow I named so that I wouldn't start thinking of shadows as bad and wrong. We. All. Have. Them. There is nothing bad or wrong about our shadows. They offer wisdom, power, and jewels to anyone who cares to go inside and look around. And if you don't heed their call, they may sabotage you so that you give them the attention they seek.

Wendy is the shadow that most informed my intimate relationships. She was born one dramatic day when my mom drove away and left me alone because she was angry with me. I was thinking: "Hey, I'm too young to be alone!" I pleaded for her return as I ran down the middle of the street after her car. My little girl brain truly thought she was gone forever. I had already been left by my dad. This was too much. I only ran about half a block, but my heart felt as if it were miles. She didn't stop. That moment secured a spot for Wendy in my life. She said: "We have to be perfect so we never make Mommy angry so she never goes away again." This quickly evolved into: "We have to be perfect so no one goes away again."

I became the perfect little girl so my mom would be happy. I did my best to hide anything that could be construed as an imperfection or a cause for her unhappiness. Since I never knew what would trigger her to withdraw her love from me, I had to be sure that I was as perfect as possible. But how close can you be to someone if you are constantly afraid of exposing an imperfection?

Oops! Did that ugly part of me just slip out of its hiding place?

This self-sabotaging message definitely interfered with my ability to love and be loved. It manifested itself in my relationships as excruciating little mantras that I was unknowingly repeating to myself:

- Be on guard. Love can be pulled away from you when you least expect it.
- Be as perfect and self-sufficient as possible. If your needs are few, you have a better chance of keeping love.
- Don't get too close. Keeping just enough distance will keep the imperfections hidden.

While I may have a strong desire to be in a relationship, Wendy has equally powerful beliefs that a relationship will unveil my imperfections and ultimately take away my freedom. Wendy loves lots of space, adores being single, and chooses men who have trouble with intimacy because she does too.

Being vulnerable with another person—particularly if sharing the imperfect parts—is terrifying for Wendy. When she feels unsafe or smothered, she will sabotage a relationship, whether she looks like the instigator or not. She's crafty, too. She can make it look as if the other person is responsible when, in fact, this little shadow bears just as much responsibility, if not more. I am an expert at picking fights that will lead to my partner retreating.

Does Wendy really want that distance? No. She wants closeness and nurturing. It's my job to know what Wendy and all my shadows *want,* and to give them what they *need.* In other words, I get to be the healthy parent to a beloved group of disenfranchised children.

I once met a man who created a shadow belief when he was a young boy working with his dad on math homework at the kitchen table. At one point, his dad grew frustrated and slammed his fist on the table, yelling: "You're so stupid!" Then he walked out of the room. That little boy became a young man who had internalized his father's judgment. He adopted the belief that he *was* stupid. He went on to earn multiple graduate degrees, trying to prove over and over, long into adulthood, that his father was wrong and that he was anything but stupid. This shadow was running his life, sadly at the expense of a personal life. Once the part of him that always felt stupid was heard, honored, nurtured, and reintegrated, he no longer needed to prove his dad wrong and was no longer driven by the pain of that seminal event. The healthy parent reintegrated the disenfranchised child. He now had the space, time, and energy to focus on inviting love into his life. It was as if he saw the world in Technicolor after living for decades in black and white. That's how powerful shadows can be.

Now, some of you may be shaking your heads and thinking: "Well, these stories are just crazy dramatic. I don't have anything like that!" But you may want to start looking back at pivotal traumatic moments (possibly split seconds) in your own childhood. Ask yourself what you decided about yourself, others, and the world in those moments. What crafty disempowering mantras did you make up? Perhaps something like these:

- It's not safe.
- I'm not lovable.
- I don't belong.
- I am wrong.
- I'm all alone.
- I'll never be good enough.
- Happy isn't for me.
- This is as good as it gets.

Sometimes these declarations are so powerful that we develop special abilities to overcome them. We create new, seemingly powerful, mantras that can be just as disempowering for our hearts' journeys:

- I am tougher than nails.
- No one can make me feel safe.
- To hell with love.
- I will pour myself into work, money, my body, spirituality.
- I decide where I belong. I will be so dominant I won't have to belong.
- I will be right from now on. I will know everything I can.

- I will amass as many friends and be as busy as I can so I am never alone.
- I don't need to be happy; I just need to be useful.

While you may get a momentary power boost from uttering any one of these statements, if you don't uncover the disempowered shadow self who first felt the pain, it's a little like putting a Superman costume complete with fake robust muscles on a baby. The power is airbrushed on to cover up the unhealed pain.

If some of the negative disempowering mantras above resonate for you, but you still don't know what caused you to believe them, don't worry. That may come with time. For now, you can start playing with these more powerful messages to start healing:

- It is safe to love and be loved.
- I belong.
- I am perfect as I am and as I am not.
- I choose happy.
- I am here now in my power.
- I am loved.
- I am love.

I use these mantras like vines to help me swing through emotional jungles. But you don't have to be in the jungle to benefit from them. You can copy one on a Post-it note and slap it on your computer or fridge. These can be safe and sacred tools for exploring your inner self. Sometimes the least sophisticated tool can do the most exacting work.

Are you starting to see how even the simplest awareness of a previously hidden internal driving force can bring you power? This is often hard medicine to swallow. For the record, I fight it every damned time it comes up. When there's something I don't have that I claim I want, there is usually something inside my subconscious, hidden from my view, that keeps me from having it. Saboteurs can suck the juice, magic, and power right out of our superhero dreams.

One common reaction we all have from time to time, which is a clue that a saboteur is at work, occurs when we take things personally. It's a rare person who has walked this earth and never uttered the phrase: "How can I *not* take that personally?" If you find yourself saying this, it likely means that your heart is hurt, that you've been triggered, and that a saboteur is clutching on to you for dear life.

When I take things personally, I feel as if my hands rush up to my chest and I cry out: "Poor me, poor heart; I must protect you!" But how can love get through if your hands are tightly clenched protecting your heart? How much responsibility can you take when you're in a defensive mode? Most important, how can you stop and dive in to look for the saboteur responsible? When you find yourself taking something personally, it's good to ask yourself some questions:

- Does your heart need protection like that? Not at all.
- Is everything always about you? Nope.

- Is it sometimes about you? It's rare, Superhero, super rare!
- Should you take responsibility for what you can? Yes.

And then? Switch your focus, Superhero. Look inside for that shadow.

When you take things personally, you are not in the present. You are stuck in the moment in the past when you first experienced that pain and your saboteur is screaming: "My feelings are hurt!" You may need some help switching your focus. I highly recommend phoning a friend to help you get your bearings.

When I take things personally, I want to be held and have a man say: "It's all going to be okay." When I told this to my friend Fran, she asked: "When else did you want a man to just hug you and tell you everything was going to be okay?"

Aha moment #359! There were many times when I wished my dad had been there to hug me, console me, celebrate me, and laugh with me when I was a kid. He and I became close when I was in my twenties and remained so until his death, but we had to get reacquainted and make a clear a path through our painful past. Our separation had been very difficult for him as well. He apologized for the hurt he had caused and explained what was going on behind the scenes that I never knew. We healed our relationship and found that, while we were on polar opposites of the political spectrum (a source of more hilarity than pain, thank God!), we were spiritual soul mates, and we grew very close.

Yet, that abandoned little-girl shadow still lives, and I didn't discover her existence until after my dad was gone. You can see how, even if you feel you have deeply healed a relationship, a shadow born long ago in the throes of a trauma can still pop up years later, hidden in the tall grass like forgotten chocolate Easter eggs. The good news is, if you crack the eggs open, even many years later, the chocolate is still really good. When you open up, look inside, and work on these shadows, you encourage your Mighty Flame to burn brightly.

My dad passed away midway through my relationship with Mr. X. I needed time alone to process all the complex feelings that come with losing a parent who is also a dear friend. Two days after my dad died, I told Mr. X I needed a night to myself. He came over in spite of my request. His presence felt like an intrusion. How could he not oblige my simple request? I felt like a caged animal and repeated that I just needed one night alone. His feelings were visibly hurt, and he said he needed me. He tried to hug me to gain some comfort, but hugging an angry caged animal is rarely a good idea.

I broke. I started to scream, demanding that he leave. I was, quite frankly, out of control. He grabbed me and pulled me toward him with a quick dance move and tried to dip me! I pulled away, asking him what on earth had made him try that. He said he had seen it work in the movies. I was wishing it were a movie so we could cut to a new scene, but I was very much stuck in this impossible moment. I was in no mood to dance, to be even slightly romantic, or to in any way take care of Mr. X's emotional needs. He finally gave up and left. I was shaking, ashamed that I had lost it, but also angry that I had been pushed to the edge.

Did he violate a boundary? Yes. Was his saboteur running him because he felt abandoned? Yes. And my own saboteur was running me. When your defenses are down, when experiencing a huge loss as I was, or even if you are just not feeling well or are highly stressed, you need to be particularly attentive to your shadow selves. They need special care during times like this so they don't have to rise up screaming for your attention in unhealthy or destructive ways.

If you can muster the courage to face your shadow selves and summon the generosity to give them what they need, you will begin to heal. The moment you can tame a saboteur within and make her feel loved and cared for is the moment you can stop pointing fingers and become loving and caring again.

The enormous gift that comes from dealing powerfully with our shadow selves is that we then have the ability to hold someone else's heart and have compassion for them and their own saboteurs. In a painful moment in a relationship, it is from this place of holding each other's hearts and allowing each other's shadows to be acknowledged that true acceptance and forgiveness can come. This is where deep love can happen. If I had dealt with my own shadow's needs, I might have been able to hold Mr. X's heart genuinely for a few minutes. And he might have been able to hold my grieving heart and even honor my need to be alone.

Holding each other's hearts is hard when you are in a relationship, and even harder after it's over. After this breakup, compassion and forgiveness came in baby steps for me. The very first step was to uncover in myself what I found so intolerable in Mr. X, which—surprise!—meant unveiling a saboteur. Usually, we protest and dig in our heels when forced to look inside when we feel wronged. When I coach women to look inside for the behavior they found triggering in their men, many say to me: "Well, that's *his* issue, not *my* issue! I would never do that. I am *not* him!"

I was hardly different, digging in with a defiant scream: "I am *not* a liar!" So, I asked the question differently: *What about lying is so intolerable to me?* Sure, none of us like to be lied to, but I had to explore why I felt powerless in the face of lies. Why wasn't it enough to just break up? Why did I still feel so much anger about the lying? Why couldn't I stop thinking about it?

I knew that if I didn't find the answer to these questions, I would find myself in a relationship with another liar in slightly more dapper clothing and repeat this pattern of deceit and pain. So, I went hunting around in the shadows.

A memory came to the forefront. I remembered when I was around the age of eight or nine preparing for my first Halloween party. Extensive plans had been made, recipes found, party games organized, and my best friends invited. Everyone was excited for the event. There would be grapes peeled to feel like eye balls in the dark, scary games to play, and caramel apples to eat. There were also bags of candy ready and awaiting party guests and trick-or-treaters—all stored in my bedroom closet.

Why my mom would put the candy in *my* bedroom closet, I will never understand. But she did. And, of course, I "discovered" it one day, and rediscovered it the next day, and maybe even the next. When confronted by my mother about the open bag and the missing candy, I lied and blamed my only sibling, our toy poodle, Prancer. Yes, I was mighty clever in my youth; the dog opened the bag and methodically took a few pieces of candy each day.

My mother decided the appropriate punishment was to cancel my Halloween party and, even worse, ordered me to be honest with my friends about why there would no longer be a party. Humiliation would be mine. At that moment, of course, I imbibed my mom's intolerance for lying and wove it into my DNA.

It took a liar with whom I was intimate and invested emotionally to shine a very bright light on that shadow created when my party was canceled. I learned through shadow work that my intolerance for lying was an intolerance for a part of myself, a part we all have. We *all* have a liar inside us. I have told lies, stretched the truth, and modified it slightly for the sake of convenience. I am a person, like most, who would rather veer away from conflict and avoid uncomfortable feelings or hurt someone by hiding the truth. So, in fact, I *am* a liar.

When I embraced the liar in me, Mr. X's lies lost their grip. He wasn't evil and I wasn't a victim. He had pain and I had pain. By revisiting that moment in time when my lie had led to great consequence, I embraced that shadow, the liar in me. It's not that I lie any less now than before; nor do I dislike lying any less now than I did before. It's just that lying doesn't have the charge it once had. The result is that I no longer draw liars into my life.

Mr. X and I allowed our liar shadows to come in handy. They helped us avoid true intimacy. We were afraid of hurting each other, so we simply didn't speak some of the uglier truths that take work to get through as a couple. Together, we avoided the real work.

I won't look at the ugly pieces of you if you don't look at the ugly pieces of me, okay?

The more shadows you unveil, the more power you gain. Imagine that, in your youth, Edgar Degas made a clay sculpture of you as a dancer. Imagine that the sculpture captures the moment of a most exalted dance pose— perhaps *en pointe*, perhaps about to leap. Now look closely at the sculpture. Notice how, as life has knocked about your heart over the years, little chunks of the clay have fallen off here and there.

The good news is that the more shadows you embrace, the more pieces of yourself you take back, the more clay you put back into place. The statue may not look exactly as it once did, nor should it. Maybe the balancing toe is gone; perhaps the graceful, floating arm isn't as high as it once was. But it is whole, strong, and elegant in a new way. For some of us, embracing these saboteurs will enable us to see that exquisite dancer for the first time. For all of us, embracing the shadows will allow us to dance far more in the light.

If all the pieces of you, shadow and light, are living in harmony, imagine what you can be to others. You become a whole and complete heart, able to accept other hearts, welcoming them in all their perfect imperfection. The following exercise can help you start to uncover some of the saboteurs that create distance between you and your own heart, and therefore between you and others. It will help you practice diving into work with those shadows. The more practice you have, the more quickly you will recognize when a saboteur is looming. The more aware you are of your shadows, the more you can integrate them into your heart. The more work you do, the more settled your soul will become and the more brightly your Mighty Flame will burn.

We all have saboteurs. Discovering them is our greatest source of power. Dealing with them consciously is the key to unearthing the greatest treasure of all: more and more love, each and every day.

Love Strong Exercise: Me and My Shadow

Think of a distinct moment in your past when you felt powerless, with no clue as to what you were going to do next—perhaps paralyzed by fear or sadness, stunned into apathy, so angry you wanted to scream, or in so much pain that you were numb. Let yourself sink into the memory of how you were feeling at that moment and identify what preceded it.

Try to remember what you looked like at that time, as if you were witnessing yourself from afar, a stranger passing by. From a distance, you looked just fine, right? You looked like your usual old self. Perhaps you wore some emotion on your face, but nothing out of the ordinary. Many people passed by you that day and had no clue what was going on inside you. Yet you were filled with a feeling of disempowerment, almost as if there were someone else—a shadow self—inside you wearing the cloak of your body.

Imagine you can gently coax that shadow to come out and reveal herself. Imagine that she very willingly appears in front of you. Describe her: body, clothing, hair, eyes, face, voice, etc. If you feel inclined, you can draw her or find the image of a character in a movie, book, or cartoon that reminds you of her in some way.

Now it's time to have a chat with her. You can carry on a little conversation in your mind or you can do what I do—write or type your thoughts. You can even record your voice. Find a time when you can have a quiet moment to honor her fully without interruption. Ask some or all of the following questions and let her answer. If you act as if *she* is typing or speaking for you, it may flow a little easier.

- How old was I when you were born?
- What event created you?
- What did that event make you believe about yourself?
- What are you still angry about? What do you still cry about?
- Is there anything you want to say to me?
- What would you like to be called? I want you to have a name that you love.
- What would make you happy now?

To conclude, you can tell her why she was created and that she now deserves the nurturing and support that she did not get at that time. And you are here to give it to her.

Note: If the answers don't flow easily the first time you try this, please give it another shot. I promise it's worth it.

Chapter 5

KRYPTONITE

The blessing is in the breaking.
That which refuses to be broken
refuses to be blessed.
It is the breaking of life that produces
the blessing of life.
Bishop T. D. Jakes, *Oprah's Next Chapter*

Kryptonite is the one thing that could bring Superman to his knees. We all have our own special kryptonite, which is anything or anyone that takes you out of your power and drowns you in the illusion that you are not loved or lovable. Of course, shadows can create that illusion. And while kryptonite can lead you to doing shadow work and may even bring you face to face with a saboteur, in this chapter we will deal with the sudden forces from outside that can disempower you: a frightening situation, shocking news, even a loving offer from a friend that ends up not being in your best interest. Some land mines are cleverly buried by our shadows; some we trip on unexpectedly. This chapter is about the chunks of kryptonite we find ourselves suddenly, shockingly clutching.

When you're healing a broken heart, you're bound to trip on some kryptonite. You will come up against people, situations, or emotions that will test you or even render you powerless. The good news is that you are about to start building your superpowers to help you handle these situations. But even now, when you find yourself clutching a chunk of kryptonite, I am here to tell you that, yes, even at that most difficult moment, you are powerful. And, what's more, every particle of kryptonite that you wrestle to the ground or throw far out into another galaxy will make you more Love Strong.

Just like our saboteurs, kryptonite itself is *not* the enemy. It is actually a blessing. Like saboteurs, kryptonite wakes us up to the places in our hearts that need attention. So let's get you equipped to deal with it when it makes its way into your hand, heart, and mind. Here are three suggestions:

- Drop the kryptonite (a cousin of "drop the mic"). Sometimes you just have to grab your power, have the last word, and drop that kryptonite!

- Watch your body. The effects of kryptonite can manifest as physical symptoms, so you need to keep an eye out for them.
- Watch your words. Words are powerful. What you say about your relationship partners, what you say about yourself, and what you say to others can all be laced with kryptonite.

You never know when you'll need to use one of these tips, but increased awareness of all three can help you stay on the path to becoming more Love Strong.

DROP THE KRYPTONITE

Several months after my breakup with Mr. X, a girlfriend called and told me that he had received a high-profile acting gig. That very simple bit of news, only several words in total, brought me to my knees. Here's a rundown of my thoughts when I heard this news. Mind you, all of this occurred over the course of approximately four seconds.

First: "Oh, look at me, hearing his name, and feeling so groovy about Mr. X. I am soooooooooo good. All healed with nowhere to go but up!"

Then: "Wow, so odd that this friend happens to be bringing me 'news' of Mr. X. What are the chances of their two worlds colliding?"

Then a proud: "Good for him! He's . . ."

To an almost instantaneous: "He's having that level of really cool, good stuff happening to him?"

And then a slightly less-immediate transition to: "OMG! What am I saying? Look at my beautiful life! I am so lu . . ."

With an immediate switchback to: "There is no justice."

To—thank god—me declaring to my friend with a big smile on my face: "I really just have no interest in hearing about great things happening to him, thank you very much!"

One piece of news and all hell broke loose. We both laughed. Really hard. Sometimes a slap of honesty is all it takes to make you drop the kryptonite. Laughing, particularly with a friend, is very healing. Don't force it. But part of the "game" of dealing with kryptonite is seeing it for what it is: a potential source of powerlessness delivered by an outside party. Drop it. Remember who you are, Superhero, and dive on in to see if there's any part of that gorgeous heart of yours that could use some healing.

After I recognized this piece of kryptonite for what it was, I got to work. I had been living in a bit of a bubble for months, avoiding contact with anyone who knew Mr. X, anyone who might tell me something about him. This incident showed me that my healing was like one giant *mille feuille*, that delicious French pastry also known as a Napoleon that looks as if it has a thousand delicate layers that will break with the slightest touch, each layer holding up the one above with the thinnest layer of the most delicious cream.

I had healed hundreds of layers, yet in the stack there were some that were still cracked—the parts of me that still needed to look outside myself for love. Those layers are just going to take a little longer to heal, and that's okay. I am fragile, and I am strong. I am wounded, and I am healed. We are all a delicious combination of neatly finished business and cracked layers of unfinished business. We are susceptible to kryptonite *and* we have a Mighty Flame burning inside. And I was going to drop that damned kryptonite.

I learned just how tightly I tend to hang on to kryptonite a few days before my birthday in St. Maarten, at about the one-year anniversary of the breakup. My friends and I arrived one bright morning at a lush and lovely jungle setting for some zip lining. I was at the ticket booth paying for our group when the woman at the register said: "You know it's not *just* zip lining, right? It's an obstacle course *and* zip line." No, I did not. But I imagined playfully jumping over low hay bales and assumed it would not be an issue for any of us. I had never experienced a real obstacle course—not that a miniature hay bale would be considered an obstacle by most.

I casually reported back to the group what the woman told me and everyone was game for the full adventure, so we suited up with our zip-line gear—which made me feel like a superhero, by the way. I highly recommend it. Our guide, Gorgeous Hunk George, explained with a stern and sober tone that we must have one of the two hooks of our harness connected to a guide rope *at all times.* He repeated it a few times as gravely as if an ambulance had only just departed with someone who had rejected his warnings. Still, I was wondering what kind of frail or challenged people needed to be "hooked in" when jumping over tiny hay bales.

George led us to a tree with a rickety ladder going up its trunk. I immediately thought: "Hmmm, that's a little bit of a scary, precarious situation." I was still in my hay-bale fantasyland version of what an obstacle course might entail.

I was leading our pack, so I was first to arrive at the landing high up in the trees, where I saw that there was, in fact, not a single bale of hay in my future. Leading from one tree to the next was a sparse wood-and-rope "bridge." When I put my first foot onto this wanna-be bridge, the whole thing started swaying from side to side. Halfway across, I heard the deep guttural tones of a man laughing. I glanced up and saw that George had somehow swiftly, magically climbed the next tree to meet us on the other end of this life-threatening obstacle. I gave him a stern look, which only made him laugh harder. I asked, with teeth tightly clenched so as to not lose any element of my grip: "Whaaaat?" He laughed and asked: "Are you cursing?"

He had seen me muttering to myself and assumed that I was swearing. I was, in fact, praying. Hard. I screamed, as best as I could through tightly clenched teeth: "No! I'm desperately repeating a sacred mantra so I won't die!" He laughed even harder. I had been doing Lamaze-like breathing until I thought I might really fall, at which point I started an incessant rhythmic chant of the Sanskrit mantra *"Om Namah Shivaya"* (translation: "I bow to the Divine"). I swear I survived because of it. George, I'm sure, would disagree. After all, I was, indeed, hooked up to the guide rope.

The next obstacle was a tightrope—a thick wire that looked as if it would slice you in half if you slipped. I was sweating buckets. The adrenaline shooting through my veins made me shaky and unsteady, and therefore even more nervous. Nerves chasing nerves, terror creating hysteria.

I got to the other side and nearly collapsed. I had considered myself to be tougher than that, more warrior-like, but I was absolutely, unequivocally terrified. Upon my arrival, Gorgeous Hunk George did his best not to laugh and, instead, mustered up a sweet and gentle: "You don't need to hold on so tight."

In that moment, I learned the lesson of the day. It seared through my soul. I won't say that the fear went away, but I do know that during each challenge after that—and the worst was yet to come—I focused on letting go of whatever I could think of that might be thwarting me. My mantra for every crossing became "I let go of . . ."

Then, in one moment, all my muscles froze. The obstacle in front of me was a series of swinging logs all in a line. You had to step gently from one narrow log to the next so as not to make them swing even more, all while suspended high above the jungle floor. As I prepared to step from the landing onto the first log, George must have seen each and every one of my back muscles tense. He put his hand on my shoulder and gave two very gentle brushes to my back to set me on my way, as if to say: "Even for this challenge, you don't need to hold on tight. Yes, even for this." I loosened my grip and made it across with far more grace than I had expected.

This lesson and George's gentle, albeit silent, coaching still echoes in me today. There is nothing and no one in my life that needs to be held onto so tightly, especially kryptonite.

Sometimes you just need to loosen your grip. Sometimes you need a friend or even a temporary coach like George to remind you. Sometimes you need to let some gentle love bump up against your heart to soften it a little, or even someone who can momentarily help you hold your heart with some tenderness when you both know it isn't at its strongest.

So when you find yourself holding on to kryptonite, use this Superhero of Love version of "drop, cover, and hold": *Drop, discover, and hold that heart!*

WATCH YOUR BODY

A few years before I met Mr. X, I had a panic attack. I was on the jetway, boarding pass in hand, ready for my flight home from Chicago. I had flown hundreds of times without incident ever since I was a child. I'd never had anything resembling a panic attack. But, on this day, the thought of being in a sealed metal tube sent me into an anxiety orbit. As I walked toward the plane, I felt as if there weren't enough air; my heart was pounding and I started to sweat. I turned around and begged the gate agent to put me on a later flight. I calmed down enough to get on the next plane, but, as soon as I landed, I started making calls.

I travel a lot, for work and for pleasure, and I decided I needed to track down a hypnotherapist to help me with the panic attack. Events like this simply weren't going to work for my lifestyle. I found a brilliant doctor who rid me of this fear in just a couple of sessions. I see now that he was working with my saboteurs. There are many points of access to calm saboteurs and to deal with kryptonite. Having a buddy—professional or not—can get you there with a bit more ease and speed.

A few months after my breakup with Mr. X, and several years after that hypnotherapy healing, I was having old mercury fillings taken out of my teeth, which required my jaw to be set in one position for a long period of time. The procedure wasn't at all painful, just awkward because I was locked into one position. But the experience gave me a hint of that long-ago anxious feeling. My subconscious worked it out that night. I had a nightmare in which I was stuck between two walls, unable to move. A very calm, wise voice repeated to me in the dream until I woke up:

If you can't move side to side, go deeper.
If you can't move side to side, go deeper.
If you can't move side to side, go deeper.

You can't solve anything by taking nervous steps left and right, back and forth. Einstein spoke about problems needing to be solved from a different point of consciousness than the one that created them. And so it is with your fears. You need to dive deeper to find the solution. You must get at what is underneath the anxiety. Or, in the case of kryptonite, get to what is disempowering you.

The trick is to calm down and be present so you can go deeper. When you are in a state of anxiety, you are either reliving the past or projecting yourself into the future, which means you can't be present to look at what's around you, in front of you, or inside you. You need to be in the here and now to get to the source of that kryptonite.

I realized with this dream that the repetitive negative thinking I indulged in about Mr. X was still playing in my head—the endless wondering about which of his words had been genuine and which had been lies. The crazy firestorms were gone, but there was this lingering repetitive thinking, a form of kryptonite. I had to "go deeper."

When I did take that dive, I saw that the kryptonite I was holding on to was the picture of what I thought that relationship was supposed to be. I was splitting my time between the past and the future. I had to bring myself lovingly back to the present, let go of the pictures of the future, and then let go of the past.

Come back, Little Sheba, your place is right here in the present. Come on, it's comfy here, I promise.

Self-care is key to clearing the way so you can go deeper; body, mind, and spirit all need to be nourished to support the work. Do what it takes for you and your body.

Sometimes I need to work out vigorously to get the endorphins going; on other days, I need to do no exercise at all. Sometimes it's as simple as lighting incense and candles to make my home feel like a temple. On other days, I need to go into the backyard to walk barefoot or lie in the grass. Sometimes calling up a friend for support does the trick; very often it's meditation that takes me the deepest.

My therapies of choice after my breakup with Mr. X were meditation, tea breaks, hot baths, and herbal and Bach flower remedies. I avoided alcohol because it depresses me physically and emotionally when I am feeling down. I didn't want to cultivate more sadness. Once in a while, when out for dinner with friends, I had one glass of wine. But even then, I knew that I'd pay for it by not being able to regain my center as quickly. Not everyone is cursed with this sensitivity, but if you are, heed your body's whispers.

The nervous dance I do when I'm stuck in repetitive thinking—shuffling left, right, forward, backward—is something I am learning to recognize more quickly. Just as I pay attention to my body's dis-ease, I try to recognize my soul's unrest as an alarm that says: "I'm out of sorts; take care of me." Sometimes my soul is screaming: "Please can I let go of this kryptonite now?" This demands a true stop, even if just for a few moments, to uncover the kryptonite's message.

Only you know what you need to do to deal with each chunk of kryptonite. If you are suffering and cannot break the cycle of repetitive thinking, please reach out for help. There is no shame, or even the tiniest bit of weakness, in seeking assistance when you are stuck. On the contrary, it's heroic.

WATCH YOUR WORDS

On the first New Year's Eve after my breakup with Mr. X, I had a party. Just before midnight, I set out paper and pens, pencils, and crayons, so that people could write or draw all that they wanted to give up or let go of from the past year. I built a roaring fire outside and people sat in a circle, some quietly contemplating, some writing furiously. For a couple of minutes, there was just silence among us, a rare quiet moment for a New Year's Eve celebration. In the silence, my friend Bob raised his head and asked: "Can *I* let go of Mr. X?"

Bob had never even met Mr. X, but he had been one of the people who helped buoy me up that first year. He told me repeatedly that I was a great catch and he really wanted to let Mr. X have it. Great friends are priceless. Great male friends who join the Love League and sometimes threaten the "bad guys" without really ever intending to do anything at all? Priceless *plus*.

You may need help from your Love League to rise above potential kryptonite negativity—people who will say to you: "You've got this." If you feel you don't have anyone like this in your life, look more closely. They may just be waiting to be asked. Ask yourself who the positive forces are in your life. Who makes you feel good when they are around?

Who makes you feel good about yourself? If you don't have people like that around you, look outside your inner circle of friends. You may be due for some new friends. For some, it's a therapist who provides this support; for others, it's an anonymous support group. Actively seek your peeps. If some friends cycle out of your life, don't freak out. That's the nature of friendships and that's the nature of transformation. They may be back. Sometimes your growth requires you to move on for reasons you'll never understand. Imagine Gorgeous Hunk George telling you not to hold on too tightly.

Finally, it may be that, in order to draw something toward you, you have to become that thing. For instance, if you complain that you have too much drama in your life and want to lead a more peaceful existence, look at how you create that drama yourself. If you complain that you don't have people who are generous with you or support you emotionally, try being generous yourself or practice being an emotionally supportive friend with others.

Practice *being* what you seek in others. If you practice being peaceful, you will create peace around you, and the drama will leave your orbit. If you practice being generous, you will be amazed at the generosity that will start coming in your direction.

Be vigilant with yourself. And make sure your Love League is on the same page as well. Tell even just one of them what you are up to by declaring your commitment to transformation: "I'm done complaining about this. I'm done pointing fingers. I'm transforming this. I am working on becoming _____ (fill in the blank)."

As friends, we sometimes fall into the trap of supporting less powerful parts of ourselves: "Oh sweetie, of course you feel that way. Everyone has let you down. It's not your fault; it was him."

I've done it and I've had others do it for me. We mean well, but we aren't serving our friends or ourselves when we use these kinds of statements. So this is my official public apology to all of my girlfriends: In the name of comforting, I sometimes did not support your highest good. Our womanly magical ways—our abilities to nurture, nourish, and empathize—can feel like a warm bath. But they can also keep us from attaining our highest good. Essentially, what we are doing with our comfort is saying: "Here, let me hold up that pointing finger for you for a while. You've been holding it up for so long, you must be tired!"

At the beginning of my breakup with Mr. X, I had everyone believing that I was the victim of a possible pathological liar. Most who had known Mr. X were shocked. Some were not surprised. My Love League rallied and came to my side to march in an anti-Mr. X parade complete with a banner. With me in the center and all my loyal girlfriends locking arms in solidarity, they marched with me down the road to recovery.

I was so grateful to my Love League for doing this for me, because, at first, I wasn't ready to assume full responsibility for my role in the demise of the relationship. I needed to clench that kryptonite and organize a Mr. X protest. I wouldn't change one part of my process and will be forever grateful to my girlfriends for every word they said during this time. They had no idea how desperately I was clutching that kryptonite. But if I hadn't dropped the protest banner that said "Mr. X Is a Liar," I would have gone through life assuming his lying was the only cause for the relationship's failure.

Another thing we say to each other when suffering heartbreak is: "You deserve so much better!" I used to say this to friends, and a few have said it to me. Even in the midst of my pain, though, it didn't sit right. The concept of "deserving" is a funny one. Who gets to decide someone's worthiness? It's judgmental no matter how you twist it. Hanging on to the thought that I deserved better was kryptonite for me, largely because it had me pointing fingers at Mr. X, not at what I needed to address in myself. So watch out for feelings of self-righteousness, which can just be kryptonite in a crystal's clothing. And it can be as disempowering as other more obvious bits of kryptonite. Self-righteousness can stop you from trying to be better and from doing the work you need to do.

Also know that the more superhero-like you become, the more loving, supportive people you will draw into your life, like moths to a flame. And you will be more drawn to love as well. Will bad things still happen? Absolutely! But I can promise you that the more work you do on building your superpowers, the shorter your periods of disempowerment will become and the more agile you will be when dealing with kryptonite.

Here is an exercise to help you with the kryptonite-laced stories we tell ourselves. Yes, we even hand ourselves doses of kryptonite. And storytelling is one of the most common ways we do this.

Love Strong Exercise: Kryptonite Stories

Think of a time when you felt as if you were holding kryptonite. Remember the time when my friend told me that Mr. X had gotten a high-profile acting gig? Try to recall a moment when you felt similarly disempowered, brought to your knees.

Write a story about the experience. Tell it like a dramatic screenplay, recounting scene by scene what happened.

You can also tell the story out loud. Just be sure to find some uninterrupted time and private space, because you don't want to feel inhibited in any way. I like recording my stories on my phone, because I find that saying them aloud frees me up creatively. Do what feels easy and natural to you.

Feel free to embellish the story; give people fancy character names; make the settings even more dramatic. Just keep the *seeds of the truth* present in the story—the basics of what truly occurred and the truth of your actual emotional state.

Refer to yourself in the third person for dramatic effect, as if you are a character you are watching on a big movie screen. You can even pick a genre. Is your story an action film? A thriller? A western? Is there music?

In other words, let your imagination run wild to recreate the experience with as much drama and flair as possible. Here is my Southern Gothic drama that helped me retrieve my power from that chunk of Mr. X kryptonite:

The year is 1945. The Second World War has just ended. Our heroine, Eliza Ledbetter Dunbridge, is at a gala affair in a lavish hotel ballroom in Manhattan. Champagne and music are flowing; spirits are high. Eliza is sitting at a table having an intimate yet light conversation with a colleague who also happens to be a friend. A third colleague, a dapper gentleman, interrupts their conversation and says to the friend: "I just heard the news that you've been named the new President of our Universe! Congratulations!"

This, of course, was brand-spanking new to Eliza, as she too had been under consideration for the post of president. When the man leaves the table, Eliza sits with her mouth agape and asks her friend if it is, indeed, true. The friend brings a chiffon hanky to her left cheek, uttering in the sweetest of southern drawls: "Why no, chile, I never heard such a thing in all my natural life! I do declare I am most certainly not *the President of this here Universe!"*

In fact, it was true that the friend had been named the President of the Universe. And so it was in that one moment, that Eliza began her descent into hell.

My twist on what really happened maintained the truth, yet allowed me to see how overly dramatic my response had been, how much meaning I had attributed to minor events, and how much I had translated these events into something about myself.

After you've written your story and included all the elements of the experience that disempowered you, there is one final step. Ask yourself these three questions:

- What really happened? In one sentence, facts only please. For example: She lied to me.
- How did it make me feel? In as few words as possible, please. For example: worthless, jealous, and sad.
- What is the "story" that I made up all about? Does it describe what I thought my actual experience meant? In other words, what is the dramatic, yet false, moral of the fairy tale you made up? One sentence max, please. For example: This proves that I am unworthy and unlovable.

Take a moment to celebrate your creativity! Then take a moment to sober up and see the truth in all its glory. We take all the delicious ingredients of the truth and bake the most disempowering cakes that we then devour. We all have a five-star disempowerment bakery nestled in our subconscious. Let this awareness help you loosen your grip on the kryptonite.

Mighty Flame Check-In #2

Are you starting to feel some sparks? Are you beginning to own your power a little more? Are you gaining confidence that you are getting ready to fly high? Rate your answers on a scale of 0 to 10—or 10 to 0. Your goal is to move your scores to the right side of the scale.

My heart pain level is about:

10 9   8   7   6   5   4   3   2   1   0

My energy level is about:

0   1   2   3   4   5   6   7   8   9   10

My obsessive thinking about my loss is roughly:

10 9   8   7   6   5   4   3   2   1   0

My joy quotient is about:

0   1   2   3   4   5   6   7   8   9   10

Chapter 6

SUPERHERO TRAINING CAMP

You had the power all along.
Glinda, the good witch,
The Wizard of Oz

Remember when we first arrived at the Temple of the Mighty Heart and tuned our ears to the whispers of lifetimes of superheroes who had come before us? It was there that you heard your Superhero of Love ancestors recognize who you are. You are one of them, a beloved.

Let us now step back into the temple. You are ready to start your training. This is where your heart will get an immediate warm-up, softening the edges that were hardened by pain and strengthening the parts that you have left unattended. You are about to find out that you are more supported than you ever knew, superhero!

Let's enter the temple for the next step on your journey to healing.

The motto of Superheroes of Love is *Ex Amor Fortitudo*—Strength through Love. The training you are about to begin will help you find your strength through the ever-replenishing source of love inside you. This training works. It will bring life to the superhero inside you and connect you to real love—the kind that can't be found in any other person, place, or thing, the love that fuels your Mighty Flame.

Can you feel the hearts of those who have come before you? They are with you now and will remain with you throughout your journey.

Close your eyes for a moment to feel the Mighty Flame inside your heart. Imagine it is connected to the Mighty Flame at the center of the temple and to the heart of every superhero who has come before you. Feel the love connecting you all, as if you are one circuit of love. Let it fill your heart with strength. You are about to make that circuit even larger as you step into your training camp. So much love and support are about to descend upon your heart!

Superhero training camp is comprised of three elements:

- The Love League, a posse you put together to help you take care of your heart
- Training coaches, the wise ones who inspire you

- Heart prep, which helps you get ready to strengthen all five superpowers

THE LOVE LEAGUE

Imagine yourself at the end of this journey, back at the temple entrance, standing powerfully at the top of the stairs looking out at the magnificent view. You are victorious; you have conquered your crazy firestorms. Your cape billows out behind you. Imagine a magical and wondrous team of superheroes filling the temple behind you, beaming with pride for you and all that you have accomplished on this journey, knowing you as a fully trained Superhero of Love. That's your Love League.

You choose who you want and who you need to be in this inner circle. You may know many of them already. Others may start swooping into your life when you begin to focus on your desire to gather this most holy team together. Members of your Love League do any or all of these things for you:

- They help you set up healthy boundaries with yourself and others.
- They support you in keeping your word to yourself and others.
- They provide a clear and honest mirror for things you may miss seeing in yourself.
- They help you hold and process your pain.

Even superheroes have to know when to enlist support. That's why the Love League is important. If you only give, your heart can only grow so much. Hearts are meant to give *and* receive. Your Love League will help you stay balanced and expand your capacity for both self-love and love for others.

My friend Ann is always looking for opportunities to be of service and she helped me see what an enormous service it is to ask for assistance. She has a playful "just ask" attitude. If you were to follow her through her day, you would think she was spreading magic fairy dust everywhere she went. What she is doing is looking for opportunities to be of service and for others to be of service to her. Sometimes people can't provide what she is seeking, but she doesn't make them feel anything less than thrilled to have been asked. Then she moves on to the next possibility to give or receive. She's an extraordinary member of my Love League.

Finding Love Leaguers who have this wonderful flow going is priceless. For some of us, the salve on our hearts is simply giving. But you have to learn to grab onto whatever makes your own heart open wider. If you are a Type A personality like me, your heart may be more stretched by receiving.

The day I moved into my house, I was suffering from a hideous flu and I desperately needed help beyond the team of movers I had hired. It took everything in me to ask my friends for help. I felt as if I should saw off an arm to repay them, and I didn't have enough arms to go around. But all my amazing girlfriends (indeed, some Love Leaguers) were genuinely delighted to come help me.

Being vulnerable is still hard for me, but it's crucial for every superhero because collaboration and community feed our powers. Sometimes you just need someone outside yourself, someone with some distance from the situation at hand, to be a little more clear-headed than you can be. Will you have opportunities to give back to them? Of course. That's the natural flow of life. But don't worry about it when you are in crisis. Allow yourself to receive the support in the moment, and let your Mighty Flame guide you to opportunities to return the support down the line.

My Love League was one of the most important elements of my healing. Right after my breakup with Mr. X, I desperately wanted to call him to berate him for lying. I wanted to ask him endless questions and hear all the sordid details behind his actions. But I knew that if I made that call, it would add fuel to the firestorm that was threatening to consume me.

So I enlisted friends to check in on me so I wouldn't have too much time alone with my thoughts. I knew that if I was surrounded by too much silence, temptation would take hold. I called people to help me fight the battle, to stop me from calling Mr. X. They doused the fires by letting me vent, by not judging any of my thoughts or feelings; they talked me off the ledge with care and empathy. They kept me from calling him.

Sometimes it took a few calls for me to reach someone, but I always managed to find a real live voice at the other end of the line and it worked every time. Most often, these calls were quite short: "No, Bridget, you don't need to do that. What could you do instead of calling him?" At first, I just needed an ear to listen to me rant a little. But beware of using your Love League to help you stay in an endless spiral of complaints. Complaints weaken your powers. Each time you choose not to complain or allow a Love Leaguer to point you in a different direction, you grow more Love Strong.

You may be surprised at who will step up to join your Love League. Acquaintances, friends of friends who have just gone through something similar, mentors from other parts of your life will all come forward if you ask. Some of them will sigh with relief that you have finally asked for help. We all want to make a difference in someone's life. Your Love League will be proud and happy to make a difference in yours.

It's a good idea to let them know what you need from them and what they should expect from you in return. It's important for both sides to be clear so that you are working toward the same goal: becoming Love Strong. My agreement with my Love League was: "I'm calling you so I won't call him."

I never called him. I'm sure there were a few times when each member of my team thought I might falter. They had to remind me often that calling him would just make me feel worse. I didn't want to lose their support by breaking my word, and they definitely did not want to see me waiver, so they supported me.

And there were times when I had to call a few people, one after another, until I felt better. After one call, I'd be fine for a while, but then I'd start to falter, so I'd pick up the phone again. Once I made it through the danger zone, I could stop calling. But know this: The storm does pass; peace does return. I promise.

Your Love League needn't be huge either. Just the act of creating your community, even if it is made up of only one, two, or three people, will help you feel fortified and supported.

If you feel as if you have no one to ask and you are in the middle of a dangerous emotional jungle all by yourself, I can tell you with absolute certainty that there will be vines to swing on when you need them. You may feel as if no one can help, but help is *everywhere*. It can come in many forms, so start keeping an eye out for the vines that get loosened by the angels and helpers and friends in your life.

The most important thing to know is that making silent promises to yourself doesn't carry the same weight as when you share them with someone else. The more you share your commitments with people, whether spoken or in writing, the better chance you have of achieving your goals.

Your Love League will be able to see things more clearly than you can at times. They can offer perspective when you are blinded by the firestorm of your emotions. Listen to them, even when you think you have a clear head. Let them be your eyes until you can see more clearly. They may even show you a whole new perspective that you haven't considered, one that will remain a piece of your heart forever.

Years ago, I was with a group of friends on a ranch in remote Idaho. Not being an expert rider, I misjudged my horse's intentions. I thought we were going to walk calmly around a bush, but he knew we were jumping over it. I flew over his head and landed on my elbow. I assumed from the sound that it was a bad break. I had to be transported by ATV to an ambulance to get to the hospital. I felt each of the many bumps on that dirt road. I was in excruciating pain. I lay there wondering if I would ever regain full use of my arm.

I started to panic, escalating my worried thoughts toward an envisioned amputation. The EMT next to me was a big, burly guy who had been pretty silent throughout the ride. Getting up the courage to ask him if he would hold my hand was harder for me than it was for him to reply: "Sure, I can do that." I'm guessing he had never been asked to do that before. He didn't look like the sort of guy who would be asked for an intimate favor like this. To his enormous credit, after a telling but brief hesitation, he very sweetly took my hand in his. After a few minutes, I could see that he felt good offering me this comfort, and I immediately felt calmed.

Sometimes we just need people to hold our hands. Perhaps, more precisely, we need them to hold our hearts. After my breakup, I divvied up the hand- and heart-holding duties among my Love League, some of whom I know I exhausted by leading them down the same circuitous path of despair over and over. They were good EMTs and kept both hand and heart firmly supported in spite of my emotional shenanigans.

You may not even see where you've been burned; you may need a friend to help you to dress—or address—the wounds. You may need someone to be straight with you and tell you something you don't want to hear in a way that you can understand—to show you that anger or sadness is getting in the way of your recovery. And it may take a friend to reflect back to you how much you've grown. That, too, is a cherished Love League duty.

Surrender to your Love League whenever you can. Practice letting love in, even though it's scary.

It's safe here.

TRAINING COACHES

When you want to learn how to play tennis, you can get any good player to teach you. But when you want to win Wimbledon, chances are you will seek out someone who has either won the tournament themselves or helped someone else to do so. So it is with becoming a Superhero of Love. You need proper coaches to back you up and show you the way.

Spend time with people you consider to be Superheroes of Love—people who can teach, inspire, and coach you, even from afar. You may have several in your immediate social circle. Some may be strangers, perhaps famous authors or thought leaders. Read their books; post their quotes around your home. Meet them and tell them they are your superheroes (own it!). Follow their wisdom on social media, blogs, TV shows, etc. You do not have to be physically in the company of people for them to serve as superhero training coaches.

I've mentioned some of my own coaches before, but their names bear repeating. I benefited greatly from the support of Debbie Ford, Ford Institute coaches, Marianne Williamson, Mark Nepo, Gloria Steinem, Anne Lamott, Gary and Linda Zukav, and Gay and Katie Hendricks. I read their books, listened to their talks, and attended their classes and lectures whenever I could. Rumi, the 13th-century Persian poet, was the coach who unfailingly breathed oxygen into my Mighty Flame by reminding me of the beloved inside me at all times, a reflection of every other beloved I would meet.

In the midst of training with all these wise teachers, I received emails from two different friends inviting me to a Los Angeles event with a spiritual leader from Australia, Master John Douglas. At the time, I felt as if I had plenty of support. Yet something told me not to delete either of the emails.

Attached to each email was a letter from my friend Ann, who had been cured of Stage-4 terminal cancer, much to the shock of USC's oncology department. She had been told she would be on chemo until she perished from that cancer. The letter, sprinkled with details of her miracle, was, in essence, a love letter to Master John.

Days before the arrival of this mysterious miracle worker, I searched online for information about him. Nothing I found really swayed me, and yet I was drawn to his website, to find whatever it was that seemed to be calling out to me.

Over here. Yes, that's right. Closer. Closer. Closer . . .

On his website, I found a link to download one of his CDs. I figured that, if I listened to what appeared to be a seminal teaching, I would have my answer. I "came to" about five hours later, my heart filled with bliss, my body and soul at peace. I had accidentally set the file to play as a continuous loop. While the process I was led through is only nine minutes long, each time it played it seemed as if I heard something new. Needless to say, I signed up for the event my friends had suggested I attend.

Master John deals with the unseen forces that inhibit us as we pursue our goals—including our own subconscious. He heals our hearts' wounds on so many levels. Saboteurs retreat like wild mustangs tamed by the glance of a horse whisperer.

In my first one-on-one healing with Master John, he found the remnants of a thought pattern that had plagued the women in my family for generations—a tendency to let minor negative events immediately result in an end-of-the-world reaction. I didn't even mention this to Master John, but he saw it as clearly as if it were etched in my DNA. He took care of it and the pattern was broken forever.

All the therapeutic, healing, and spiritual work I have done in my adult life has been aimed at tuning in to my intuition and being more present. I give credit to all my teachers and healers for moving me closer and closer to my goal. I also believe that we happen upon the great teachers in our lives in the perfect order, at the optimal moments. Master John came to me when I could receive what he had to offer. His healings have brought me to a place where my soul is humming, most often singing, and I can hear its song now because there is far less chatter obscuring it. He says: "Your song is LOVE FM! Stay out of CRAP FM."

I know CRAP FM very well. If we could all stay tuned to LOVE FM (every Superhero of Love's favorite channel!), imagine what this world would look like. Master John answers this query for us: "Every particle is singing a song of love. When we change our song, the world corresponds."

If you don't resonate with Master John's work, you can simply explore in your own way his simple recommendation to uncover your song of love and rise to your highest potential. It helps to have someone who has already risen to those heights who can help you navigate the journey up, up, up. There is no shame in following a teacher. Wise teachers provide us with the means to scale the heights more rapidly and maximize our superpowers. Just keep your eyes and ears open. Ask the universe to bring you the coaches who can help you step into your own special powers. The perfect ones will come, I promise.

HEART PREP

It feels easier to shut down your heart for business when it has been wounded. But putting a "closed" sign in the window doesn't stop people from trying to enter. And the bad news is that, when you shut others out of your heart, you shut yourself out as well. Your heart may be weak, burned out, and not ready for prime-time superhero-dom. This part of your training will help you become more Love Strong by helping your heart to be more open, resilient, accessible, soft, and courageous. You'll accomplish this through two important practices: heart strengtheners and heart openers.

Heart Strengtheners

If you're going to climb Mount Kilimanjaro or compete in a marathon, the training you have to do is intense. One common technique is called high-intensity interval training, also referred to as HIIT. This method is exactly what it sounds like—a workout based on intense periods of effort performed in short intervals. For instance, if you are training in cycling or running, you sprint hard for a few minutes and then resume a normal pace for a minute, then sprint again, and then repeat the pattern. The intervals shock the hell out of your system, raise your heart rate, and cause your body to burn more calories long after your workout is complete. These are superhero workouts to be sure.

If your heart is recovering from a loss, particularly if you are in the depths of pain, you may find yourself doing another kind of interval training called High Intensity Interval *Heart* Training, or HIIHT. It's not walking. It's not jogging. It's a high-intensity regimen that combines rest periods and sprints in a pattern that will build and test your strength. Half the battle is being aware that you are in training and that you are asking something significant of your heart. If you are conscious of it, you can get the support you need and come out the other side even more Love Strong.

Inhale. Exhale. Then what? Inhale again? Oh, okay. Thank you for the reminder.

We need to have compassion for our hearts as they work out. The essential difference between normal interval training and heart interval training is control. At the gym, we purposefully craft the sprints and rest periods of our workouts to suit our goals. In life, on the other hand, we are thrown into the high-intensity periods of our workouts with no warning and must strive to catch a respite here and there.

Here are some things you may be saying that can indicate you are in high-intensity mode. The sprint may feel as if it will never end, but you can be sure a respite is coming.

You will start noticing where you are as you listen for these markers.

You're in a breathless sprint when you find yourself saying:

- No, no, don't leave me!
- This can't be the end!
- I can't stand not talking to him.
- I haven't been alone for so long I don't even know who to be, what to do, how to act!
- I'm mad I lost friends to him.
- People don't understand what he did to me.
- I can't let go! I don't want to let go!

You're in recovery mode when you find yourself thinking:

- I am grateful for the time we had.
- My heart is more at peace when we don't speak.
- I am growing accustomed to my own company again.
- I know my bounty of friends will replenish. New friends are coming. Good old friends will always be there.
- I take responsibility for my part in this.
- I am finding some peace in releasing the pictures of what I imagined our future would be.

High-intensity interval workouts at the gym are usually accompanied by music that leads you through the ups and downs of the journey. You work hard through the choruses because you know they won't last long. You steadily work through the less arduous parts with songs that build in intensity and orchestrations that make the journey almost exalting.

Yes, we can! We can climb the impossible peak!

A soundtrack for your heart workout can be helpful as well. Listen for it. Find an anthem that will help you climb the hills. Alicia Keys's *Streets of New York* made me feel I could "make it" when I felt out of emotional steam. Andra Day's *Rise Up* always makes me feel as if someone is shouting at me: "You've got this!" Katy Perry's *Firework* is always good for a final sprint and helps me take flight. I wasn't even conscious of what Perry's lyrics said until I was on the other side of my rough patch. She is a Superhero of Love who acknowledges the firework that is inside each of us—the mother of all sparks, the Mighty Flame.

When you become more conscious of the intervals, the ups and downs you'll go through in this healing process, you end up taking better care of yourself. Life doesn't always stop at one loss or one crisis. Sometimes these experiences are piled on and you think that you simply cannot sprint up one more mountain.

One week, I was nearly consumed by loss. People and animals all around me were coming to the end of their lives, each fighting to hang on. It was also the birthday week of my dad and my grandmother, both of whom I had lost in the few previous years, as well as the anniversary of the death of a dear friend. I felt as if I were climbing Mt. Everest in a snowstorm without oxygen. The heaviness in my heart was so great that I couldn't breathe. I felt as if my heart had to grow bigger than my body, as if it were expanding outside the confines of my chest.

To survive this moment in time, I had to become bigger than I had known myself to be in the past, to be present with all the pain and intense love. This high-intensity period truly made my heart grow. I realized that I could love even more expansively than I had previously thought. I could be present with people in emotional pain without needing to fix it or take it away.

And just as I thought that I couldn't take one more bit of pain, more came and I found that I *could* do it. I didn't break. My heart expanded. But I also took care of myself; I didn't do anything extra. I was in the "extra" zone already. For these high-intensity heart workouts, you may need a flame-booster kit, an emergency pack to help you take extra-good care of yourself, to soothe and calm your aches and regain your power. Even superheroes need a bubble bath every now and then! Only you know what you need to have in your kit, but it may include any or all of the following:

- Sustenance. I needed to add extra sleep, more hot baths, and even homeopathic remedies. I needed to pay attention to my water intake to keep my energy up and clear.

- Relief. I needed to ensure that I didn't go above and beyond the call of duty or I risked giving away too much of my energy. My tolerance for alcohol goes down when I'm running on emotional empty, so I cut it out completely during rough patches.
- Free passes. Write some for yourself, actual ink-on-paper permission slips to sleep in really late, order take-out for dinner, play hooky from work or another commitment, or take one day or even a week off from pursuing a goal that you work on every day.

You have to stay even more awake and clear when you are climbing the big mountains. So plan for those mountains. Start thinking of what you need in your flame-booster kit. Here are some signs that some self-care may be in order.

Thoughts you may be repeating:

- I can't.
- I miss him.
- I don't know which way to turn.
- I can't go on like this.
- He's the only person I want to talk to about this.
- I'm afraid for my kids.
- I don't know if I'll make it on my own.
- I'll never stop dreaming about him.
- I can't stop thinking about him.

Feelings you may be experiencing:

- Sadness
- Confusion
- Resignation
- Resentment
- Despair
- Fear
- Doubt
- Hopelessness
- Obsessiveness
- Feeling you are doomed

When we break up, no matter who initiates it, we experience waves of emotion—grief, sadness, anger. While those waves can be big and powerful and knock you down, they do ebb. You have to acknowledge the ocean's power, but also trust you have what it takes to stay afloat. When I lost my dad, I learned to take the waves of grief as an opportunity to stop and be with my immense love for him, to honor him with my memories, and simply be with and inside that love.

One word, scent, or song can send you adrift after a loss. A waft of Indian food sent me out to sea one night. I was right back at a favorite restaurant that Mr. X and I frequented. I avoided driving through that neighborhood for a long while, for fear of the waves. I wish now that I had just ridden them. I wish this for you as well, because avoiding the waves means avoiding the ocean where you can also swim and play, or float peacefully, basking in the sun or moonlight. Even though you may feel as if you will drown if you enter the waves, I am here to tell you they will not take you down. You have a Love League that can throw you a life preserver. In the next chapter, you will learn how to hone your superpowers so you can surf these waves and come out the other side of your pain.

If we don't deal with our emotions, we are susceptible to getting sick in some manner, either physically or mentally. Most of us know someone who has grown chronically ill after suffering a great loss. We can see that they are not only stuck emotionally, drowning in grief or anger, but they are also suffering physically. Pushing feelings down by over-eating, over-drinking, over-exercising, or over-anything doesn't stave off the feelings forever either. It just makes us look and feel terrible!

In her Shadow Process Workshop, Debbie Ford likened avoiding our feelings to trying to hold a beach ball under water. At some point, your arms will get tired and that big ball of suppressed emotions will rocket into the air. If you wait until you are in the middle of your next relationship to deal with the pain—well, good luck with that! That beach ball will probably hit you in the face in the middle of a romantic dinner when your new love says something perfectly innocent. But when you brave those pain dips, ride those waves, and take care of yourself, you cannot help but become more Love Strong.

Heart Openers

An open heart is a mighty heart. When your heart is an open channel through which love can flow in and out, it becomes a giant power generator.

In my quest to heal my heart and chisel away at the cold, stone barriers created by past pains, I gravitated toward sweet, warm remedies, like the poetry of Rumi. Rumi wrote about the beloved, who can be perceived as both God and a lover. This focused my attentions on God, Spirit, and the purest of loves that makes my heart spring back to life by opening those love channels. I kept a Rumi book with me at all times during my healing to inspire me to remain open-hearted as he was, open to God and to the hearts of others.

Another superhero training coach who always offers a salve for my heart is Marianne Williamson. I participated in her Enchanted Love Workshop, throughout which Marianne led us in guided meditations and conversations to help us create a more sacred relationship with love. In one, I saw myself standing, shielding my eyes with my right hand while forcefully stretching my left arm in front of me palm up, as if to say "Stop!" to anyone coming toward me. Yet in the vision, it wasn't a person from whom I was shielding myself. It was a bright light. I knew in that instant that the light was supremely divine—God, my own light, and all the love I had ever pushed away. And I realized that that light is always inside me. It is the Mighty Flame, the source of infinite love, and the place where we are and always will be Love Strong, no matter what.

Then another wave of realization washed over me. While I had been keeping the light at bay, I was also shunning the dark, denying both myself and my loves the opportunity to heal those dark places we were brought together to explore. Superheroes have to be able to dance in the shadows and bask in the brightest of lights. Nothing taught me this lesson more clearly than a visualization Marianne led in which we were instructed to think of someone we had loved in the past, or imagine someone we were yet to meet. Then she led us through the intimate ritual of bathing each other's feet. Having been to India several times, where I learned about the sweet ritual of bathing a master's feet, my heart burst open. The mere thought of treating a love in this way—understanding that he and I were masters for each other, potentially leading each other to a higher place—was very moving. Imagine bathing the feet of your love as gently and lovingly as you would bathe a newborn baby.

Deep into this visualization, I envisioned something that can only be described as otherworldly. Mr. X and I were beings of light. There were no hard edges defining our bodies. In my mind's eye, I reached my hand gently into his chest to touch his heart. I very delicately took his heart out of his chest and poured warm water over it. In fact, this felt more like pouring my own love into it. I just calmly held it, feeling more and more love each second. Then I put it back and we were both, as a result, even brighter lights.

This visualization revealed one of the most powerful Superhero of Love lessons: When we give gentle love to each other's hearts, we make our own Mighty Flames grow stronger. Imagine what the world would be like if we treated each other's hearts and our own hearts with such care on a regular basis, honoring our mutual vulnerability. This is what ultimately makes us Superheroes of Love. In giving, we receive; in receiving, we give. And each expands our hearts' capacities.

Some say that the term "open-hearted" is a misnomer, that our hearts are never really closed, just as the sun never ceases to shine. The question is not whether your heart is open; the question is how much light is in your heart. For, if it's closed, no light can get in.

It feels good to be warm.

We tend to build some pretty strong stone walls out of the hard and crusty remains of past losses. Experiencing the softness of love can feel as impossible as hearing music coming from a soundproof booth. We rub up against the hard edges and don't recognize that even these self-imposed borders don't have to be as rigid as we make them out to be. We have the power to soften those edges so we can feel that love. And, it's a natural instinct to shield ourselves from the stabs. It's actually kind of incredible that we haven't evolved to have tortoise-like shells over our hearts. It would be hilarious if we could see each other's otherwise invisible shells as we meander through life: Oh that looks like a doozy of a heartache, poor guy. How is he able to drive like that? He must have really long arms.

One of my friends had her heart broken when she was a teenager. To this day, in her forties, she has not re-opened that door. Another friend in her sixties is in the same spot after a man left her for a younger woman more than twenty years ago. We all have our tortoise shells and steel doors. But what do superheroes do with barriers? We bust through them!

We leap over the tall buildings of our anger; we dive deep into the seas of our sadness; we jettison ourselves across the grand canyons that our saboteurs have carved; we fly high with our hearts to touch as many other hearts as we can!

If you're unsure whether your heart is more closed or open, the following lists of markers will help. Here are some things that people *say* that may indicate a closed heart:

- I will never get married again.
- I'm done with dating.
- I don't need a man in my life.
- All the good men are taken.
- I'm just not interested in love anymore.

Here are some things that people *do* that may indicate a closed heart:

- Avoid social interactions
- Freeze or lose steam around dreams and goals
- Reduce phone calls to friends and family
- Rebuff compliments or attentions that encourage them to get back in the dating game
- Over-focus on their children's lives or work

I knew my heart was opening on a morning that began with subtlety and grew in force. I had just come back from the farmer's market with my bounty of flowers and veggies. The flowers were particularly joyous—an array of ranunculus, mini calla lilies, gladiolas, and daffodils. I made arrangements and placed them all around the house, starting at my favorite Buddha statue. He was particularly happy with the offering. I shared his joy and sat down to meditate. I usually struggle to wrestle my chatterbox self to the ground. Sometimes it's a matter of letting my thoughts, negative or otherwise, come and go as they please until they simply lose their power. Most often, though, I focus on a mantra that I can cling to like a magic carpet.

But when I am already filled with joy, I am clear, connected, and present. I feel lucky, as if wishes can come true. Since I was already in this state when I sat down to meditate on this particular morning, I asked for a message. This is what I received: To receive love, your heart must be soft like the heart of a flower.

I imagined opening up a flower to look at its center. I didn't want to hurt the flower, even in my imagination. So instead, like the sperm that made their way swiftly toward the egg in the movie *Everything You Always Wanted to Know About Sex (But Were Afraid to Ask)*, I imagined swimming down into the heart of the flower. I dove into its center. It was soft and warm, this place where the joy of being a flower resides, where its reason to be remains until it is no longer. I knew that this is where a flower's inspiration lives, the place that tells it to turn its face toward the sun, to reach its roots into the earth, and to open its petals.

In our own soft, warm, fluid hearts, we likewise find the source of what draws us toward the warmth of love. It is as pure as the instinct to turn to the sun. This is a spot that can be felt and heard. When something touches this place, or you hear it speak to you, you know it's the truth. The more opportunities you take to touch it, the more you will be able to "be" with it, tap into it, and live it. And the more you live it, the more Love Strong you will be.

It's hard to open your heart and hear this truth when you are living in fear. Swami Chidvilasananda (Gurumayi) taught me that all choices lie either on the path of love or on the path of fear. Life choices are as simple as choosing between apples and oranges: you must choose love, not fear.

This wisdom has come in handy for me over the years. Usually, I can discern the path of love and avoid the path of fear. But I've also developed an uncanny ability (like most humans) to disguise my fear, wrapping it in a fluffy cloak that looks suspiciously like love. We have all seen people rush into a new relationship before fully ending another because they are afraid to be alone. Yet they truly relate to the new relationship as a choice of love. While sometimes these can end up being long-term, loving connections, often the fear of being alone can drive us toward something that is not truly love.

Is that love in fear's clothing or fear in love's clothing?

Even though I had been single for a few years before I met Mr. X, I see now that I jumped into the relationship because I was afraid I wouldn't meet another man who would value me, or whom I considered to be so much fun. I had also hard-wired an alarm clock into my brain that I didn't even realize was ticking so loudly that it was challenging my clarity: "Must be married before fifty or you'll just be an old dog lady."

While I would have sworn that love was driving my choice to be with Mr. X, there was a lot of unconscious fear guiding me. Fear put the blinders on and covered up the things that would have otherwise been deal-breakers for me in any relationship.

Let your fears rise up so you can look at them with open eyes. Understand them and evaluate them with an open heart. Whatever you are afraid of is rarely as ugly as you make it out to be in your mind.

I turned fifty and I didn't self-combust because I was single.

Your Love League and superhero training coaches will remind you of these facts: To fear is human, and even the most colossal of fears won't take you out. More important, having a hot and juicy relationship with fear can lead you to have the courage to see, to dive in and confront a truth you may not have seen otherwise. If you can go one step farther and transform fear into excitement, fear's not-too-distant cousin, you may discover a direct path to the other side of whatever frightens you.

It's mighty vulnerable work uncovering these fears. It takes attention and courage to remain open-hearted. So if you are feeling less than brave, try pumping some empathy iron. At the beginning of my journey, when I was most in pain, I often wondered about how many other people on the planet were suffering the loss of a love in exactly the same state of mind at that precise moment. I remember being curled up in bed, traveling the world in my mind, imagining someone on the other side of the globe suffering a broken heart just as I was—a person weeping in Sweden, someone begging God to relieve their pain in Nairobi, a man pouring his heart out to his girlfriend over coffee in Naples, a woman in Japan staring silently at the ring her lost love had given her.

I could muster up some mighty empathy for my imagined brothers and sisters. I wouldn't dare belittle what they were going through as I did with myself. Sending loving thoughts to others in my situation brought me comfort. We are all in this experience of life together. We all love so similarly, from the flutterings, sighs, and tinglings of new loves, to the straining, piercing, and blood-letting that can punctuate their endings.

My friend Ann once shared some wise words with me about compassion. She said: "When we are trying to get somewhere, we have to have compassion for ourselves. Like when we are trying to lose weight but the pain of not eating and feeling hungry distracts us from the fact that the pain will lead us to a higher place." You have to have compassion for the part of you that is instigating the special breed of pain that will allow you to step into your greatness.

The superhero's path must be paved with compassion—for ourselves, for our bodies, for our powers, for our loved ones, for our enemies. We often treat ourselves with even less compassion than we give to our enemies, don't we?

I have one hell of a saboteur that feeds on my lack of compassion for myself. When you make a decision at age five that you have to buck up and be your own parent, you become a pretend grown-up with distorted ideas of what being a perfect kid should look like. I have friends who had this feeling as kids as well. We all developed some pretty kick-ass shadows. Type A personalities often have a shadow running the show, cracking the whip, making them feel as if they are less if they don't deliver stellar results. God forbid we fail or falter. But man, can we get things done!

No matter how strong any of us appear on the outside, though, we all lose touch with *terra firma* from time to time. So take this tip from me, your first coach: Sometimes you just need to fake it 'til you make it. At the right moment in time, faking it can be both a heart strengthener and a heart opener. You may not feel like smiling, or even crawling out of bed. You may feel as if you are drowning in negative emotions.

Let's talk about the worst-case scenario. You don't want to engage with life. You feel as if you have a cloud around your head. I was there. Unfortunately (or fortunately!), like most people, I had to function during the week. But the minute the weekend hit, I was just a useless lump, lying in bed, wedded only to Cary Grant movies. I made a pact with myself to accept every single invitation I received. Usually, I rushed out to fulfill the obligation, distracted by my pounding desire to get back into bed with my beloved Cary. Yet, by joining the real world, I did my soul a lot of good. When you go out with people, you practice letting love in and giving it back. That's an excellent exercise for a charred heart.

Another little fake-it-'til-you-make-it tool is to imagine being a Superhero of Love and feeling like that superhero, with all your powers at the ready, your Mighty Flame roaring with passion. Try this exercise to take a step into your greatness.

Love Strong Exercise: Superhero Sweet Spot

Batman has his cave. Superman has his phone booth. Every superhero needs a sweet spot where they can suit up in peace. Well, Superheroes of Love can suit up anywhere!

Being able to transport yourself quickly in your mind to this place of peace will come in handy. It can help shift your perception and turn a disempowering moment into an empowering one.

Think of someone—from your life or from history, or a character from a book or movie—whose power you revere. Someone you would love to meet if time, place, and money were no issue. Think of those with whom you want to spend some time to learn the secrets of their powers and the places they go to empower themselves. For example, maybe there's a special chair or throne they sit on for a moment, a meditation place where they start their day, a secret garden they retreat to for solace, an elaborate walk-in closet where their suit awaits them, a special car, a magic carpet, a grand balcony with a spectacular view, or the beach just outside their door. In your mind's eye, watch them dress and prepare themselves for the day.

Now move further into your imagination and conjure up your own sweet spot, a place you can go to to escape when the crazy firestorms start to envelop you or a place where you remind yourself to keep an open heart.

Write down some details of your special spot. Use a journal, or even record the details by speaking them aloud so you can come back and listen to the story of what you've created in your mind's eye. If it's a spot you've actually been to, you can use a photo. If it is somewhere you have longed to go, retrieve a photo of it from a magazine or online. If it's in your imagination, create a collage of all its elements or find one photo that sends you there. Keep this representation of your safe, secret place.

This is your special place. No one else can enter this unique spot. Nor can anyone ever take it away from you. Go to this place when you feel you need a power boost. It is there for one sole purpose: to bring you back to your superhero center.

Chapter 7

THE FIVE SUPERPOWERS

You're much stronger than you think you are.
Trust me.

All Star Superman Comic Book #10

Now it's time to work on your superpowers. I'll introduce
the five powers and give you an exercise for each one so
you can really step into that power and feel it in your heart.
This is where I get to prove to you the presence of that
Superhero of Love inside you. This is where you get to take
another step toward superhero flight. The work you have
done up to now has cleared your heart and readied you for
this.

The exercises are designed to build your superhero muscles gently, like the short runs you do at the beginning of

marathon training. When I started training for the one and only marathon I ever ran, a very cool thing happened. As I started feeling stronger and extending my tolerance for longer distances, I became more invested in the process. For instance, before I started my training, I had never run more than ten miles. I'll never forget the day I ran twelve, a distance that had previously sounded impossible to achieve. Once I did it, two things happened: I trusted that the incremental increase of the distances I would have to run would be manageable, and I became more invested in the journey and unwilling to give up on this big dream. As you start working with these superpowers, I hope you will become invested in being even more Love Strong and won't want to quit either.

This momentum is what carried me through when I found out that Mr. X was married. I didn't want to fall back into the abyss of negativity, judgment, and powerlessness. I wanted to get back on my superhero track as soon as possible. Yes, I stumbled a little, but I regained momentum quickly and was feeling even more powerful in no time. It was a serious workout with a lot of steep hills and a lot of deep breathing, and I made it.

No one arrives at the Temple of the Mighty Heart with all five superpowers fully developed. You may have a natural inclination toward some of them and may have been honing others since you were a kid. You were probably even an expert with some of them as a child. Others may feel brand new. I started meditating when I was twenty-one, so my

Super Hearing was pretty good when I started this journey. I knew how to listen for guidance, but I also had a helluva lot of internal negative chatter going on, so I had a lot of work to do on that aspect of Super Hearing. I didn't seem to have Super Sight at all; looking at my saboteurs was a whole new game for me. Even if you come to a superpower and think you've got it wired, I invite you to look at it with some innocence. Our hearts have been bandied about over the course of our lifetimes, and one inclination we humans have is to put on the equivalent of horse blinders so we don't quite see the whole picture. If you set those blinders aside and approach this work with an open mind, you may find more juicy sources of power.

So, let's get this superpower party started!

SUPER SIGHT

Super Sight allows you to shed light on the darkest places in your heart, see previously hidden saboteurs and sources of kryptonite, and use your eagle eye to perceive opportunities to love and be loved.

One thing I knew for sure when I started this journey was that, if I had been with someone who consistently lied for two years, there were some dark places in my heart that needed some very bright lights shone upon them. I created this mess, and I needed to look around and find out why. Until I could find the lights, I fumbled around in the dark.

I can't see anything in here. Where am I?

Then I realized that I could actually turn on the lights to see what was previously tucked away in the shadows. I could do that. I had control over the lights. If I turned my attention toward the shadows—voilà, instant light! The mere act of looking shines the light on that which is hidden, that which may be endlessly, silently stripping you of your superpowers.

Do I really have to go in there?

If you are afraid of the dark, throw on a cape, grab a flashlight, and pretend you have no fear. As I said earlier, faking it 'til you make it will at least get you in the door. Then, as you actively brave those shadows, your eyes will adjust to the dark and that Mighty Flame will soon start to shed the light you need to look around.

My dad often repeated a phrase that made me laugh every time I heard it. When I told him something, his smile would grow into a grin as I spoke. At its peak, each and every time, he would say with eyes dramatically open: "'I seeeeeeeeeeee,' said the blind man."

I see the whole thing. I see. Inside. In. Sight.

The first step to developing Super Sight is to look at what is true right now—to see the present moment in all its glory, without blinders or hands covering your eyes. If you have a habit of hiding out, shielding yourself from both your shadow and your light, this can be tricky. I'm here to coax you out of that self-imposed closet, to tell you that the light on the other side of the door is breathtaking. Nothing is as dark as that closet. If you feel certain you will perish if you face the pain directly and take the dive into the shadows, I must warn you: A saboteur is running the show.

We all have things we don't want to confront. Confronting saboteurs can be even harder than challenging a loved one, especially if it was born of a trauma or painful childhood wound. If you are afraid of "seeing" something inside that you think will cause you to spiral into a depression, please reach out to someone you trust with all your heart. All. Your. Heart. You have to feel safe on every step of this journey, but some steps require assistance. It's also a good idea to ask your Love League if they think you are avoiding anything, as it may be affecting your Super Sight.

Another thing that can trip you up is a powerful attachment to ideas about what you think you should have, or things you used to have. It's often very difficult to adjust to relationships as they change form. Even when you have long departed from someone's life and know you will never see that person again, you have to be able to see that the relationship is still present in your heart. It has merely changed form. Renowned Buddhist monk and philosopher Thich Nhat Hanh tells us that love and death don't have the hard-edged borders that we want to give them. He says that we are more like clouds than anything else, ever changing our form from death to life, life to death. Hanh speaks of the lover who seeks her departed beloved, encouraging her to think of the beloved in the form of a cloud: "A cloud can never die. A cloud can become snow or hail or rain, but it is impossible for a cloud to pass from being into non-being."

Hanh encourages us to hear that beloved call to us: "Darling! Darling! Don't you see me in my new form?" (Oprah's *Super Soul Sunday*, May 6, 2006).

The day I heard those words, I experienced a lovely synchronicity that brought the lesson into my heart a little more deeply. A dragonfly came into the house and alighted on the wood floor just a few feet in front of my desk. As soon as I saw it and found it was still alive, I removed the dogs from the room so this beautiful, shimmering creature wouldn't be scared away. I assumed that it was in some distress, since it didn't fly away when I came to examine it. It stayed in that place for hours as I worked away at my desk, remaining quietly aware of it. At the end of my work day, I moved it out of harm's way to the leaves of an orchid plant. I thought the beautiful flower canopy might prove to be a nice hospital for him. I sensed he was not well, since he moved his wings very slowly and allowed me to transport him to safety.

The following morning, I returned to my office to find that, indeed, the dragonfly was no longer alive. I took him outside and buried him beneath a rosemary bush. I thought it was a bad omen that such a magical creature had died in my home. I had never seen a dragonfly in anything less than flight-worthy, dazzling shape. But I felt lucky that he had come to my house and allowed me to love him a little before he died.

The dragonfly was not our only insect angel that particular week. A katydid visited for several days, simply perched on top of the flat-screen TV. About an hour after I buried the dragonfly, I passed the TV and saw that the katydid was doing just fine. In fact, it was doing better than fine. It now had a teeny tiny bright white something next to it. I paid it no mind, thinking it was just a speck of dust. A few hours later, I noticed that there were three more teeny tiny bright white somethings, and the first one had now taken on the shape of an infinitesimally small katydid. It was a she, and she was having babies!

Death one hour; magical life the next.

I realized that if I looked at the death of my relationship with Mr. X straight on, with my eyes fully open, I could transform how I perceived it in my heart. What had been a leaden pain was now a big fluffy cloud, the wind simply moving through the more solid form that our relationship used to have, creating something new—something that would change again and again and again. With Super Sight, I could see a lost love's new form.

In my youth, a friend accused me of being a Pollyanna, ever the optimist. And I was—unbeknownst to both of us, of course—lacking Super Sight. She said I was always looking through rose-colored glasses, and she was largely correct. When it comes to relationships particularly, I err on the side of interpreting things positively, assuming the best in people and expecting that any painful accommodations I make will pay off in pleasure. She was right to accuse me of being afraid to look the truth square in the eyes. I didn't want to see the whole truth and nothing but the truth, so help me God.

I also had a pair of black-and-white "glasses," inherited from the women on my mom's side of the family. When something bad happened, it was the end of the world. This affected my Super Sight. I wasn't present in any moment of distress. I was unable to look at the truth of what *was* in order to solve the issue at hand.

I had my rose-colored-pretend-everything-is-beautiful glasses. And I had my black-and-white-end-of-the-world glasses. I also had a third pair of glasses that would have been perfectly lovely eyewear had they not been covered with the debris of past pains. I was looking at the future through the thick layers of pain from my past. Every time I was hurt, disappointed, or suffered in any way, the glasses gained a splotch of mud. Yet I enthusiastically yanked them out of my back pocket and walked around as if I could see perfectly clearly.

What dirt?

Right before I broke up with Mr. X, I went to the optometrist to have my eyes checked because I felt as if I couldn't see as sharply as I used to. My prescription needed only minimal tweaking. My glasses were not the problem. I couldn't see clearly because I didn't want to. Those dirty old glasses had grown comfortable.

Remember how I described my moment of reckoning that got me onto this journey—when I caught myself wondering what lies the man across the street was telling the woman he was kissing? That twisted translation of a romantic moment was brought to me by those dirty glasses.

As a Superhero of Love, you will more readily notice when you have accidentally thrown on the wrong glasses.

Super Sight requires you to clean all your glasses. You need to be able to see all the obstacles so you can leap over them like Superman leaps over tall buildings. You need to be able to see the saboteurs so you can walk right up to them, examine what they have to offer, and gain wisdom.

Sometimes we can't even see ourselves clearly in the mirror. If we could, we might see the reflection of long-ago hurts. This is another reason why we need our Love Leagues and our superhero training coaches. Even the wisest among us needs help to see what is hidden from our view.

There is a well-known fable of two monks who are on a long journey on foot when they come to the bank of a river and find a distressed woman. She needs help crossing the river. The elder of the two monks sees that the only option available is to carry her across. He gathers her up, makes the crossing, and sets her down on the other side of the river. She thanks the monk and goes on her way. The monks continue on their journey as well.

Hours pass before the younger monk, unable to contain himself one moment longer, suddenly cries out: "How could you *do* that? We are not allowed to touch women!" The elder monk patiently replies: "Hours ago I carried a woman across a river and left her on the opposite bank. You, on the other hand, carry her still."

Haven't we all been that younger monk? We've made up stories and interpretations because we can't see the situation clearly and we hold on to those stories for dear life. The pain is only ours to relieve.

I had brunch with a friend and was reminded of this tale. I had arrived half an hour late because there was a bad accident on the two-lane road I traveled to get there. As soon as I arrived, I made a conscious decision not to ruin our brunch by complaining about my trip. It was an easy choice to make because of the glorious oceanfront setting. We were surrounded by beauty, and just seeing it helped change my state of mind. I left all the tension of the drive and negative self-judgment over my tardiness with the valet. When my friend and I sat down at the table, he spent the first several minutes complaining about someone who had cut him off on the freeway on his way to our meeting. This incident had happened two hours before I joined him.

As I listened to his story, I thought of the two monks and started to judge my friend, pointing my finger at him in my mind's eye. Then I applied it to my own life, because I know that any time I recognize someone else's "stuff," I get to claim it as my very own deliciously icky stuff as well. If he was still carrying that trespass in his heart, what was I still carrying? As my friend went on and on about the bad driver, I amused myself by contemplating what complaint I was hanging on to. I was shocked to find out that, after many months of healing, I still had resentment about Mr. X's lying. There was more letting go for me to do.

This is what we do with our past upsets. We carry them around. We often have a many-layered, half-ton load of past loves and another half-ton load of past upsets that we balance like circus performers. That's quite a lot to carry.

God forbid we drop the past, eh? Can you imagine how much energy and vitality we would have if we didn't carry that weight? Superheroes of Love need Super Sight to see the invisible burden in their arms, so they can let go and give and receive without impediment.

There are many ways to deal with how your past is affecting your present—or worse, how it is crippling your future. Some choose psychotherapy, psychiatry, or hypnotherapy. If you haven't done therapy before, I recommend it, because a good therapist can be a built-in superhero training coach who can work on all your superpowers with you, especially your Super Sight.

Years ago, after a different breakup, I worked with a therapist to help me get out of the repetitive thinking loop that I tend to slip into after a relationship ends. He gave me two gems of advice. First, he said with utter disgust: "Why would you want to be with someone who doesn't want to be with you?" I was flabbergasted by the plainly stated truth of the matter. No story, just the facts. It was the exact slap in the face I needed.

Wake up: He doesn't want you!

It was just brutal enough to make me open my sleepy eyes. Find something that resonates for you that can help you look in the mirror and clearly *see* the weighty stuff you've been schlepping around.

And if you need a slap in the face to wake you up and keep your eyes wide open, I offer you these sentences:

- He is not choosing you right now. And you are not choosing him right now. So, who are *you* going to choose?
    - The good news: You get to choose how this all turns out.
    - The better news: If you choose you, you're on the road to becoming a Superhero of Love.
- He is gone. That is what is real right now. That's a fact. Steer yourself back to the present of what is real, right now, this moment.
    - The good news: In the present, right here, right now, you have you. You are whole, no matter how broken you may feel.
    - The better news: Right now is the absolute perfect time to love yourself.
- He didn't want to fight for you. If someone doesn't want to fight for you, they are not yours. People fight for what they want.
    - The good news: You get to fight for you now.
    - The better news: You are worth fighting for, so put up your dukes and get ready to fight for love, Superhero!

The second gem the therapist gave me is a fantastic tool to use when you find yourself longing for your ex-love. Every time you think of that person, visualize a stop sign with your mind's eye. That stop sign is the signal for your subconscious to get off the road to pain. When healing a broken heart, we tend to veer toward depleting, life-sucking, and depressing thoughts that pull us into the hell of despair with repetitive negative thinking and ever-deepening resentments. That pain does not serve us. It only dims the flame we need to fuel our recovery.

Super Sight helps our eyes stay open and clear, committed to uncovering that which is hidden from our view. The mantra for Super Sight is:

I have the courage to see clearly.

With Super Sight, you will be able to see your world and your role in it as it truly is. You will be able to look yourself in the eye and know your own power. Here is an exercise to help you look inside with courage and see the truth.

Love Strong Exercise: The Woman in the Mirror

Look in the mirror. Go through the following statements one at a time, then look yourself squarely in the eye. No blinders, no dirty glasses, no filters. Crystal clear. Open eyes.

- Name three judgments of your ex-love that you would like to let go. (For example, "He is a liar.") Look inside yourself. Do you have these same qualities in you?
- Name three qualities you would like your future love to have. Look inside yourself. Do you possess them?

Bravo! It's by looking bravely and honestly inside our hearts and seeing clearly what is there that we prove we have Super Sight. We all have negative and positive qualities. If we don't become conscious of the negative ones, the saboteurs, we will continue to bring people into our lives to help us become aware of them. And if we don't see in ourselves the positive qualities we want to find in others, we need to look at what is keeping us from having them and find opportunities to breathe life into them if they are only faintly present.

SUPER HEARING

With Super Hearing, you will be able to hear your inner voice speaking the truth about how profoundly loved you are—wherever you are, no matter what the circumstances. In the middle of the loudest, craziest emotional situation, it gives you the courage to steer clear of anything that muffles or mutes your hearing the truth.

Does a tree falling in the forest make a sound if no one is there to hear it? Or more important, Superhero, can you recognize yourself as loved without someone else to confirm it for you? That's a tough one, isn't it? The work we are doing will train you to hear the internal hum of love, the whispers of "I am loved," as much as possible. As children, most of us knew very well how much we were loved. As we aged, though, the sounds of love were muted by other signals that we assumed meant the opposite. Our "rational" minds grew louder than the still and quiet whispering of that inner knowing. We assumed the louder voice was supreme. And so began the bad habit of ignoring our instincts in favor of our grown-up intelligence. Our inner brilliance was run over by the monster truck of rationality.

What was that *about? I never saw* that *coming, I swear!*

We also need to hear the red flags flapping in the wind—a subtle, but important sound. They are not obvious warnings, like sirens, but they are powerful indicators of danger. With Super Hearing, you will hear those red flags flapping in the high emotional winds and trust the voice that speaks through the noise clearly warning you: "I'm sorry, my dear, he is not 'the one.' Next, please!" And you will want to listen to it. For it is the voice of your heart.

You have to hone your listening skills, so that you can hear the strings of your own heart amid the cacophony of sounds around you. When you first hear a symphony, it is hard to discern the sound of the violin among all the other strings. But if you've listened to someone play a violin, or played a recording of that single instrument, you are more likely to discern its signature sound.

If you have never meditated before, I am going to ask you to try it now. Meditation allows the whispers of your heart to come through more clearly by quieting your mind and clearing the noise that muffles those whispers. If you've meditated before, you're familiar with the distractions that plague most beginners. Here is a typical inner monologue that can arise, booming in your head as soon as you sit down to meditate. It can be so lively that it can even feel like an actual conversation:

I can't sit still. I don't know what I'm supposed to be doing, but this doesn't feel right. What if the phone rings? Did Maggie really mean it when she said that? How long am I supposed to do this? I really do not get this. I had way too much coffee today. Why did I drink so much coffee? I feel as if I'm jumping out of my skin. Seriously, what did she mean when she said that? I'm thirsty. I'm too wired for this. Oh, that itches! Maybe I should stop now and give it a try later, after I've calmed down a little. I have to call Maggie. If I don't call her right now, I know I'll lose my mojo. This meditation thing clearly doesn't work.

The point of meditation is not to obliterate these thoughts, but to let them flow like a movie or an old ticker tape, clicking along until they lose their steam. Watch them. Let the emotions connected to the thoughts roll on through as well. If you observe them, they will lose their power and slowly recede from that room in your head. Over time, your thought-wrangling capabilities will increase and sitting down to meditate will be less of a wrestling session and more of a peaceful allowing.

There are many kinds of meditation, and the sky is the limit with techniques. I know a few people who love

Transcendental Meditation and some who love mindfulness meditation. Guided meditations are great as well, because they use words and images on which your mind can focus. I most often use Master John Douglas's recordings, as you don't have to "do" anything but listen to them.

Seek and ye shall find the perfect meditation technique for you. When you find the right fit, it won't feel like work. It will clear away all that is holding you back in mind, body, and spirit. It will bring you peace and light you up.

The more you clear away internal chatter, the more conscious you will become of the words that come out of your mouth. What you speak is a direct translation of all that you hear—whether it's internal or external input. And boy, are we epic translators! Our tendency is to interpret our life stories into dramatic works rivaling the most entertaining novel. If you ask a good friend about the themes that are present in most of your stories, you will probably gain some insight into what will empower you. You may learn that you're always a victim, a Little-Miss-Sunshine-All-Is-Perfect-Look-How-Happy-I-Am person, or that you always forecast doom and gloom.

Start listening to the stories you tell about events and differentiate them from the actual facts of those same events. Here are some possible facts:

- He divorced me.
- I lost my job.
- He lied to me.

Then the translations:

- He's an idiot.
- It's unfair.
- He's a bad person.

And here are some possible stories you may tell or believe about yourself:

- I'm unlovable.
- I'm a loser.
- I'm worthless.

When I found out that Mr. X had been consistently telling me lies from our very first phone conversation, I made up a big story about that—what it meant about him, what it meant about his feelings about me, and particularly what it meant about me that for two years these lies went undetected. I had to repeat the following list of facts consciously, and stay out of the story I was making up:

- I met Mr. X and liked him.
- I really liked the fact that he liked me.
- I liked him more and more over time and soon I fell in love with him.
- I loved our travels and adventures.
- I am grateful that he helped me through my dad's passing.

- I found out he had lied, and I broke off the relationship.
- After the relationship ended, I found out about more lies he had told me.
- I am grateful it's over and grateful it happened.

Notice that nothing in the above list is about *his* feelings. I have no idea what his true feelings, intentions, or motivations were. Only we know our truth. So stick to the facts as you know them, with nothing made up or even conjectured.

Look here: right in front of you. What's over there is none of your business. Stick to the facts, Ma'am.

You can imagine the ugly saga I made up about Mr. X at the beginning of my healing. It's not even worth repeating, because nothing your imagination can make up will be nearly as bad as what I created. No one can be as creative as we are with our own stories. I found it very comforting to bring myself back to the facts. And I try to remember that the stories I make up never make me feel good. Ever. Seriously, never.

This is why Super Hearing is crucial. It's human to make up stories. It's super-human, super-heroic, to be able to hear the truth amid the chatter, to listen for your own truth, for the divine truth in the midst of the muck.

In seventh grade, I switched to a small private school in Pasadena filled with brilliant and wealthy people. I was on a scholarship, knocking elbows at the lunch table with future rocket scientists. I was in over my head in every way. So when a teacher made me feel comfortable and at home, as if

I could fly in spite of my shortcomings, I was ever so grateful. Luckily, several of my teachers made me feel this way. One particularly inspiring person was Tim Blankenhorn, a high school English teacher. Mr. Blankenhorn introduced us to "fire writing," a tool to open up our creativity and put us in touch with our own unique voices. I knew I would never be a Hemingway, Fitzgerald, or Yeats, and I felt that if I couldn't be great, I didn't want to write.

Until Mr. Blankenhorn, that is. He instructed us to not worry about how well we wrote and even to forget about grammar and spelling for the moment. He wanted us simply to write and see what happened. Most important, as I remember it, we were to have fun! Without all the normal pressures that come with trying to be great, I found that I truly enjoyed writing for the first time.

Years later, my dad took fire writing to a new level, as a tool to get in touch with the Divine. He told me about his own writings, through which he felt he was, without effort, receiving messages from God. (Yes, this was before Neale Donald Walsch!) He read me some of his writings and encouraged me to try his version of fire writing. I have been doing it ever since, whenever I need guidance or inspiration. Over the years, I opened my writings with "Dear Angels." Then, as I became more comfortable with it, I opened with "Dear God." After my dad passed away, I started with "Dear Dad," because I was throwing my line out into that divine sea to try to connect with him and his specific kind of guidance. In the end, the most important gift fire writing gave me was a connection to my truest self and the divinity within me. It developed my Super Hearing decades before I even knew what that was. It allowed me to hear what I lovingly refer to as my "inside voice."

Now certain of our remaining deep connection, and with time having passed to close the abyss, I address the whole lot of spirits, gods, and angels who are helping me from the beyond. To me, it's all God. I still write to my dad as a way to touch base with his spirit and see if there is anything he wants to say. The following is an example of what I receive when I take the time to tune in and ask Dad if he has any messages for me.

Thank you for the acknowledgment. It isn't necessary, though, as you have always been connected to that voice. Your problem was always the little aggravating thing we like to call "noise" on this side. Noise is always created by humans. We create our own noise over here in the form of music, lullabies, wind, loving trembles, sighs, babies' joyful cries, and laughter.

But, the noise you created—that I would admonish you for—was the noise of busy-ness, the I have to and I should, the gotta do this, gotta do that, gotta prove this, gotta prove that. I gotta show him, gotta show her.

You even wanted to show me, of course, as every son or daughter does. You want to show your value. Yet, in the showing of the value, it's like putting on a big musical when all you have to do is sit on an empty stage in an empty room and simply sing. You don't need a set, costumes, instruments, or even an audience. You just need to sing for the sake of singing, for the sake of allowing the Divine to come through you and out into the world. You simply have to be and allow your gifts and talents and true self to come through.

Pushing and pulling your talents or your self to come through a certain way takes your power away. The noise dilutes the power of your voice. And so it is that you are getting to the true superpower of hearing—allowing the noise to stop. Clear the stage, strip the room, and simply allow the song to erupt. That is God's song heard with God's ear.

Clear the decks. Pull out the plugs, brush away your hair, cup your hands around your ears, and listen to that faraway sound that is right inside your heart. Inside you, here, now. That is the superpower of love.

You and I may never know the truth about the origin of the words above. I can only say that, when I open the channel to communicate with my dad, I have the vivid experience of him dictating to me as if he were whispering directly into my ear. I feel his casual, familiar presence as I type. But, like the concept of God—like anything that we can't touch, see, feel, or explain with scientific method— your own experience and what it feels like in your own heart is all you will have. The good news is that no one can touch that. It is yours and only yours.

If there is someone you have lost, someone with whom you still feel connected, work on your Super Hearing with that person. Perhaps you have thought in the past that you heard guidance from him or her. You can practice listening to your own inner guidance with the Mighty Flame Booster, Divine Messages, given at the end of the book.

Super Hearing helps you hear the voice of your intuition, guidance from the Divine, and your own truth. The mantra for this superpower to help you stay on track is:

I hear the wisdom. I hear the love.

The following exercise will help you hone your Super Hearing and may also help you transform your relationship with someone you have lost. When you transform one relationship, it affects all others in a positive way by clearing away any noise or debris between your two hearts.

Love Strong Exercise: The Conversation

Visualize a bridge in your mind. Imagine yourself standing on one end. Now imagine that the person from whom you want to separate energetically is standing on the opposite end of the bridge. Walk slowly to the middle of the bridge. Visualize the other person walking toward you, meeting you half way. Once you make eye contact, tell the person what you are feeling. Say whatever you need to say. Let the person say whatever he or she needs to say. Take a moment to make any apologies or gestures of forgiveness that you feel may help either of you move on with grace and love. Ask yourself if there is anything else you need to say. Ask your former beloved the same. Take your time to allow images and words to flow gently into your mind's eye.

When all has been said, tell the person that you are going to cut the invisible cord between you. If the person agrees, imagine cutting that cord with scissors or anything else that your imagination suggests. If the person does not agree, you can choose what to do. Either say with love that you are going to cut the cord for your own well-being, or ask to meet again. This is your mind, your heart, your journey, so just allow the story to unfold.

Say your good-byes. Turn around and walk off the bridge.

Note: Whatever the outcome of the conversation you hear in your head, it is perfect. You may *think* you know what the other person will do, and yet you may be surprised. Even if the other person remains on the bridge after you have left, it's okay. He or she may not be as ready to be disconnected from you, and it may take some adjustment to get used to being outside of your energy. I had to do this exercise many times before I felt the cords were truly cut. But each time I did, it was beneficial, no matter what the outcome.

SUPER HUMILITY

Newsflash: There's something bigger than us out there. If you can only wrap your head around the sun being bigger than the earth and bestowing its gifts upon us, that's a start. But if you can touch an even bigger source, you will make that Mighty Flame grow even brighter. In the touching of greatness—God, Spirit, Source, or whatever you want to call it—you can find a place to bow to its magnificence and recognize that this magnificence also rests in you. When we bow to another, we bow to a magnificence that is bigger than our personalities, our histories, or our possessions. That is humility and it is priceless.

The ancient mystic poet Hafiz teaches us this lesson most eloquently: "Even after all this time, the Sun never says to the Earth, 'You owe me.'" When we have Super Humility, we allow the greatness of something bigger than ourselves to enter our lives and we allow our own greatness to shine on others. And we also allow their greatness into our hearts more easily. Super Humility softens the heart more than all the other superpowers.

The summer after college, I enrolled in an acting program, and I thought I was falling in love with my teacher. But I had a boyfriend and my teacher had a girlfriend, so I knew that couldn't be what was happening. Yet I felt an undeniable attraction between us. One day after class, I went up to him, practically grabbed him by the collar, and said: "What is going on between us?" We both knew that what was happening was odd and highly charged. He was confused as well. Yet he answered in a flash of clarity, although seeming to doubt his own words as they left his mouth: "Maybe I am supposed to introduce you to this meditation that I do." The minute he said it, I knew he was right. I felt it with every cell of my body.

Time passed and he didn't follow up on his invitation, so I began to grow frustrated. Now that I knew the source of the energy between us, I wanted to get to it—fast. I asked him where his meditation place was and, right after school that day, I sped over to this mysterious spot. I pulled up to the front of the building with my radio blasting, parked in the no-parking zone, and popped in to grab a brochure and take a peek. I didn't even stop to close the sun roof, and I certainly didn't slow the pace of my nervous gum chomping. I practically skipped in, so proud of myself for having taken the initiative to get myself there.

I showed him! Ha!

The woman at the front desk gave me one of the sweetest smiles I had ever received. In that one unconditionally loving, knowing grin, I could see my own reflection—wired and slightly crazed. The sound of the screeching wheels of my car just moments before echoed in my brain. I wasn't even in my body. She was my opposite: peace and tranquility. I felt immediately at ease just standing across the counter from her.

She gave me a brochure and, as I started to walk away, ever so gently suggested that I go into the meditation that was in progress: "You can even sit at the back, right near the door, and leave when you feel like it."

I was a little scared, but I also couldn't resist. I wanted what she had. I walked into a darkened room filled with people, each seeming to be slightly aglow, bathed in the most gorgeous dark-blue ocean of light. I plopped down onto the thick carpet just inside the door. It felt as if I were on a pillow, but it really was just carpet. The temperature was divine, as if I had been cloaked in the softest, warmest blanket of love. There was a faint smell of incense. A harmonium and a sitar buoyed up the mellifluous chanting. How did they sing so perfectly in unison? Even the people to my left and right—distinct, yet exquisitely harmonized. All the sounds, sights, and smells became one blue ocean atop which I appeared to float. I had never felt so calm and deeply peaceful in my life.

I was hooked. I meditated for a year and a half before I was able to meet Gurumayi, the spiritual teacher whose practices I learned at that meditation center. I yearned to meet her, as if my thirst could only be quenched by being in her presence. I already had plans to move to New York City to attend acting school, and I couldn't believe my lucky stars that her main US ashram was just a couple of hours north of the city.

I was so excited to meet someone who lived, breathed, and emanated the energy I had only tasted. As soon as I was settled in school, I made plans to visit the ashram. I will never forget our first meeting. I felt her energy before she even entered the room, as if a river of love flowed ahead of her. This is the way it is with great beings. They start opening your heart even before you lay eyes on them. She seemed to recognize me, although we had never met. I certainly knew her, for she had come to me in meditations many time before.

It was standard practice at the ashram that, before you met the guru one-on-one at the end of group events, you were told to follow the protocol that had been followed for millennia—sit on your knees and lower your head to the floor so that it is below your heart. You can bow like this, or lie prone.

The first time I was in the line to do this, I was scared and self-conscious. I thought it might feel disingenuous. It was so foreign to me—bowing to anyone, let alone someone up on a little stage. Surprisingly, there was not a cell in my body that did not want to bow once I arrived at the front of the line. There was something about being in front of pure unconditional love that humbled me in a way I had never before been humbled. My body, mind, and spirit wanted to honor it. It was unequivocally natural and strangely fulfilling to bow to her. My heart was filled with humility in the face of a magnificence that extended far beyond her body and form—or *any* body or form, for that matter.

Bowing to a guru is not about being less than him or her. It is a way to pay homage to that which is greater than yourself and all of us—that which is inside each and every one of us, that ultimate love or Spirit or God that is the source of the original Mighty Flame. It took me many years to take this understanding one step further. I need to bow to everyone in this manner. The greatness in me bows to the greatness in you. And this includes my love relationships. What if I had done this with all my past relationships? What if we had done it to each other? Think of what this would do to each partner's Mighty Flame.

This poem, which I call *The Golden Truth,* came to me one day when contemplating this thought:

Bow to You
as you bow to the Divine.
Bow to Me
as you bow to the Divine.
Bow to your Heart
as you bow to the Heart of the Divine.
Bow to my Heart
as you bow to the Heart of the Divine.
If we both Bow,
We are Golden.

While living in New York and attending acting school, I couldn't wait tables as most starving artists did because I am clumsy as all get out. Luckily, I had the great fortune to land a job at a major law firm. The person hiring paralegals and proofreaders had the wisdom to hire actors, writers, and artists who had recently graduated from universities but were not yet earning their livings in their fields. It was the junk-bond era—the era of massive corporate mergers, with hordes of money being spent and made. So this prestigious firm was as busy at 3 a.m. as it was at 3 p.m. This often let me work for a few hours prior to going to acting school, which was only blocks away from the firm.

The law firm took good care of us. They sent cars to pick us up or take us home if our shifts were late at night or very early in the morning. I could wake up, call the car, quickly take a shower, get dressed, and hop in the car just in time to be at work by 5 a.m. But one fateful day, my alarm did not go off. It had worked every day up until then, and it worked every single day thereafter.

On this day, though, my wake-up call was the sudden feeling that I couldn't breathe. I awoke with a start, face down on my pillow, a hand over my mouth and nose, with a knife in my back and a man whispering in my ear: "Shut up, shut up, shut up." He didn't want me to utter a sound because he thought there was someone sleeping in the loft above me. I lived in the tiniest apartment in the history of mankind. Sharing it would have been beyond grim, even by New York standards. The loft above was where I usually slept, except on summer nights like this one when the heat rose up to make the loft unbearable. I also usually had my windows locked, but not on this night.

Once I realized I wasn't dreaming, I was terrified. For a few minutes, I thought I would likely be raped and thought my chances of being hurt by the knife were also quite good.

The intruder flipped me over and I saw him register my fear. He smirked, clearly empowered, which made me even more scared. I then had the distinct feeling that I had left my body and was up near the ceiling looking down at my-self. That was the exact moment when I felt a fleet of angels crowd the room. I had never felt the presence of an angel prior to this moment. I didn't actually "see" any angels or spirits in my room; I just felt their presence. I knew I was protected and that, against all the odds of what appeared to be happening, I was going to be fine.

I calmly started to talk him out of raping me and answered all his questions about jewelry, money, and all he might steal with a coolness that only angelic help could have mustered. I told him that he didn't need to hurt me, as I was giving him everything he asked for. Miraculously, after some negotiating, he did indeed leave without harming me.

At one point, though, right before he left, he demanded the code for my bank card. I gave it to him. It was S-G-M-K-J, which is an acronym for the Sanskrit phrase *Sadgurunath Maharaj Ki Jay*—literally, "Hail to the Master who has revealed the Truth to me," but originally translated to me as "I bow to the guru—within and without." He got confused by the odd acronym and yelled: *"What is it?"* This time, I lied and told him it was M-I-L-K. It must have been obvious that I was lying. I must have turned beet red as I said it, but he didn't catch the shame and doubt that washed over me.

This trauma was my first palpable experience of celestial support, of *knowing* that support in every cell of my body. I knew I was not alone with this potentially very dangerous man and that I was supremely protected—no matter what the outcome. A peace came over me, a knowing that there was love—invisible to my eyes, but within reach.

There is love and support available to us 24/7. It usually sits just outside the realm of our comprehension. It's why people pray. They feel it. You may not need to have a dramatic experience to know it, but it helped me that I did. I haven't doubted it since, and remembering it keeps me humble. If you have felt something similar to this, tap into that feeling of humility when you can.

If you haven't experienced this kind of support, you may have experienced it in another way. You may feel humble around particular people in your life, or perhaps you had an experience of awe that touched you. Open up that tiny door in your heart where humility lives and see if you can increase your sensitivity to it in whatever way presents itself.

Gratitude is a great Super Humility strengthener. Indeed, gratitude itself implies humility. It's behind that same little door in your heart. My first attempt at gratitude for Mr. X was bogus. It was more of an unholy attempt at domination. I claimed I was "grateful" that my life was no longer impacted by his lies, that we hadn't entangled our finances or lives any more than we had. In essence, this line of thinking was self-righteous, casting him as the bad boy whose clutches I had escaped.

It took me a while to get to genuine gratitude, where I understood that neither of us was better than the other, that we had simply been perfect for each other at a certain moment in time. I am now truly grateful that Mr. X gave my personal evolution a jetpack loaded with ever-replenishing fuel. Had it not been as deep a betrayal, I wouldn't have been spurred to learn the lessons I needed to become a Superhero of Love.

When I am in a state of gratitude, I feel Love Strong, as if I can fly above anything that feels less than perfect. This is sometimes easier said than done. Believe me, I know. It's easy to slip away from Super Humility and into resentment. But it's a muscle worth working. Choose gratitude. You will fly higher, Superhero.

Gloria Steinem is another one of my unwitting superhero training coaches. She's a Superhero of Love who has taken her Love Strong self to the streets for generations of women. She once said: "I was in a taxi going downtown . . . and I suddenly thought, 'You know, I don't want anything that I don't have'" (*Now What* podcast with Carole Zimmer, October 20, 2015). Imagine being perfectly content in this moment right now with exactly what you have, loving your life exactly as it is and exactly as it is *not*. Don't argue that, if you were Gloria Steinem, you too would want for nothing. Gloria is just like us. She has followed her heart every step of the way to challenge how America—and the world—views women. That battle has never been easy. And life happens to her as well. Her heart has been broken. She had a great love who left her life far too soon. Yet in that quote, we see that she covets nothing.

It can be very difficult to have a sense of well-being. Being here, now, instead of in a constant state of wanting something different than what we have is a challenge. I am not saying you shouldn't have dreams, aspirations, or goals. But the more grateful you are for your life exactly as it is, the higher you will fly and the quicker your dreams will come true. If you feel depleted or are having a hard time mustering gratitude, start with the little things like food in the fridge and your body working its magic moment by moment.

If you start to practice loving your life now, you will manifest what you want in your life. When you hate the present moment, you are energetically pushed away from it. Your arms stretch out with hands up, as if to say: "Stop! I don't want *that!*" If you start practicing gratitude for the present, those arms will—energetically—relax and open, with hands reaching out to receive whatever you want to flow into your life.

And if you are really pissed off at life, or you're just having a hard time being grateful for what you have, try acknowledging someone else—for something they have done in the world, for something they've done for you perhaps, or for what they have meant to you and why you hold them dear. Acknowledging people makes both parties feel good.

When I was twenty-one, I had the great fortune to visit a Save the Children village in Sri Lanka. One day while walking through the village, I had the chance to interact with a group of local kids. Most of them were walking barefoot on the dirt roads. Even though their bodies and clothes were dusty, the village was well-ordered and lovely, and the kids seemed truly content. They were particularly happy to have visitors. While we were walking, I happened to see a bright red thread on the ground. I picked it up, dusted it off, and made a bracelet out of it for one of the little girls. She was so thrilled that I immediately looked for another piece of thread, hoping to make another kid happy. Miraculously, I spotted one. The kids joined in the hunt for things that we could make into bracelets. The joy it brought them created a buzzing magical energy in all of us, as we shuffled around searching for potential jewelry-makings on the ground. Gratitude can be contagious and transformative. And, boy oh boy, does it do a Mighty Flame good!

Appreciating beauty is another way to tap into Super Humility. Go out into nature, make a flower arrangement for your desk, or stand in front of a beautiful painting in a museum. Appreciating beauty enables you to bow to the magnificence of something awe-inspiring outside yourself, and can be a remedy for an aching soul. Studies show that beauty can inspire us and make us happier. Laurie Anderson tells us her husband, Lou Reed, said this as he lay floating in their swimming pool the day before he died: "You know, I am just so susceptible to beauty."* When we have Super Humility, we too can be susceptible to beauty.

One of the indulgences I enjoy every day in my home is fresh flowers. As a Superhero of Love, you mustn't wait for others to give you flowers. Treat yourself. You deserve them. Flowers provide a medicine that heals most hearts. That's why we take them to patients in hospitals, why we give

---

* Waldemar Januszczak, May 18, 2016, *http://www.waldemar.tv /2016/05/boy-this-is-it-this-is-all-we-have/*.

them as romantic gifts to awaken that piece of our heart that leaps like a frog when least expected.

Super Humility is a master heart-softener. When you have this superpower, your heart is more easily touched. The mantra for this superpower to help you stay on track is:

> *My heart is open to the touch*
> *of seen and unseen magnificence.*

Only you know what gives you the feeling that there are forces greater than yourself at hand. Maybe it's holding a baby, volunteering to read to those in hospice care, or tending a garden. If you have never exercised the Super Humility muscle in your heart, here is an exercise that will help you give it a go.

Love Strong Exercise: Humbling Words

The following phrases are powerful words of affirmation that can pull you into Super Humility.

- I am that. This is the first translation of the Sanskrit mantra *So ham.* When you say "I am that," you say that you are the magnificence, you are the divine source. If you choose to use the Sanskrit version, it is often suggested that you repeat the "so" as you inhale and the "ham" (pronounced "hum") as you exhale.

- Love is here. We can't remind ourselves of this fact too often. There's nowhere to go to find love: it's right here, right now. This is a Superhero of Love mantra you can use in any situation. Becoming fully present to love's here-ness is perhaps the most important gift you can give to yourself and others.
- I am loved. Sometimes people who have a hard time with the concept of God or Spirit can wrap their heads around feeling loved either by those alive now or those who have passed away. If this will make you feel cloaked in love, try it.

SUPER SELF-LOVE

Consider the possibility that we are here together on this mighty jewel of a planet with a common mission: to love more. Imagine that, before we were born, we were given an assignment by a divine loving source: "You're going to go learn about love now. That's your number-one job down there. Enjoy!" And then, just as we are about to drop into this earthly existence, we get the divine hilarious after-thought from above: "Oh, and for god's sake, that includes loving *you!*"

When we have Super Self-Love, we are empirically more able to love and be loved. The flow of love is unfettered.

But how do we begin the self-love journey? My answer to this question is simple: wild-ass self-acceptance. Radical acceptance of myself, or others, never sounds like an easy task, so I like to think of it more as riding a bucking bronco—hence the qualifier "wild-ass." Wild-ass self-acceptance can feel something like that. I try to stay on that bronco no matter how hard he bucks with this mantra: I am perfect exactly as I am and exactly as I am not.

The steadier I am in accepting myself, the deeper my Self-Love. The steadier I am in accepting myself, the steadier my acceptance of others. After all, they are just reflecting back pieces of me.

The most spiritually advanced people are those whose feathers are never ruffled by seeing themselves reflected in someone else. That's what happens when your buttons are pushed. You see your own traits—selfishness, greed, or jealousy—in the person you are judging. You may either have tried like the devil to stomp out that aspect of your personality, or you may simply have pretended it isn't there. For instance, bullies really push my buttons, yet I have a big bully inside me. I try to hide the bully Bridget behind the full skirt of sweet Bridget, but she jumps out from time to time. I am most aware of her when I am triggered by a bully. What is my first instinct? Bully back!

Everybody we come across is essentially holding up a tiny mirror, saying: "Hey, look at this thing in me; it's also in you." And we hold up a mirror for them that says: "Yeah, for sure, and don't forget this thing inside you that I've got in spades—the one you will go to your grave claiming you don't have. Ha! It's inside you right now!"

It's not easy. But man oh man, as with most things that require substantial effort, the payoff is extraordinary. Being on the path of wild-ass self-acceptance is part of the journey to Super Self-Love. And, it all feeds the Mighty Flame.

Now it's time to take the plunge and fall in love with yourself. We've all likely heard this advice: You have to love yourself before you can love another. It's everywhere. And for good reason. We have to start with loving all the pieces of ourselves so we can love all the pieces of others—both shadows and light. Whatever route you take to begin this new romance with yourself will be a holy one. The quest to love yourself is the divine trail that leads right back to your Mighty Flame.

When I was in college, I had the good fortune to spend my junior year in Paris along with some of my dear high school friends. It was a lifelong dream come true for me, one I'd held since age five when my grandma gave me the book *This is Paris* by Miroslav Šašek. And it was an exciting adventure for all of us. We paired up to find housing, because it was far easier to find an apartment to share. One day, I found out that the friend I had paired up with had found a place with someone else. I was devastated. I felt alone and worried that I might not find something affordable.

I did a lot of hotel hopping and couch surfing while I diligently searched for the elusive studio for one. I will never forget the dark, rainy night that I was forced to change hotels to save some money. I had food poisoning. It was raining. I opened the cab door in front of my new, cheaper hotel just in time to throw up on the ancient cobblestone street. I was freezing, was running a fever, and had no clue how I was going to get myself up the looming stairs to the hotel lobby.

If you are going to hit rock bottom, Paris is quite a lovely place to do it, but I had never felt so alone before. That horrid moment—feeling cold, sick, and alone—lit a fire under me. I knew I had to buck up and get an apartment. And I knew I had to ask for help. I went to the most powerful woman I knew in Paris, a mentor in our program, and enlisted her support. Within days, I had a perfect studio in my favorite neighborhood. What had felt like a disaster—being the odd man out—ended up being the biggest blessing of that year. I ended up in the perfect living situation, in the perfect neighborhood, with the perfect Parisian grand-mère for a landlady. I came to realize that I wasn't *un*supported, that I could get my act together and ask for help. Overcoming that near disaster made me feel good about myself. Then the *pièce de résistance:* living alone gave me the space and time to start falling in love with myself.

At home, I had always been surrounded by friends or talking on the phone incessantly with them. In Paris, I didn't live near any of my friends, the phone was super-expensive, and we were all very busy with our studies. So I ended up spending a lot of time alone. I will never forget when I learned my first Super Self-Love lesson. I was stepping off a bus, starting to walk the two blocks to my apartment after a long day of gallivanting around the city, when I thought: "Wow, I just spent the entire day with just me, and it was fun!" In that moment, I learned that I was a fine partner in crime and that I could enjoy adventures and misadventures on my own.

That, my dear, was a rollicking good time!

Even though I was an only child, this understanding that I could enjoy my own company was a revelation—and, ironically, an enormous gift from the city dubbed the most romantic place in the world. I will never dispute Paris's wily ways with the heart.

Mr. X and I had been to Paris twice, and it was delight-fully romantic both times. A few months after we broke up, I had to go back to Paris for business. I had a hard time imagining being there without someone to kiss, but I ended up falling madly in love with the city in a way I never had before. One day, I went to three museums. No companion would likely have tolerated that, but I happily devoured a walking feast of art, craving the nutrients found at the Rodin Museum, the Musée d'Orsay, and the Louvre.

Must feed my hungry soul.

Paris is the city that first taught me Self-Love, but you don't have to leave the country to learn the lesson! Perhaps there is another city or another experience that will do the same for you. Maybe it's a class you will take on your own or a restaurant you will try. Perhaps you will discover yourself when learning how to paint, to dance, or to knit. Maybe a poet or an author will tap into your heart in a way nothing and no one else ever has before. The more people, places, and things you can identify as soul-nurturing, the happier you will be—whether in or out of a relationship.

A friend once told me his therapist's advice: "You have to soothe and heal your own wounds. You cannot go to your partner for that." I have heeded that advice and shared it ever since. Imagine a relationship in which both people take responsibility for healing their own wounds. You don't come together as broken pieces looking for glue; you are two whole pieces who come together to be an even more vibrant healthy couple.

Superheroes of Love set and keep healthy boundaries. When you find that you are reaching outside yourself for that nourishing glue, and you are loosening the edges of those healthy borders, it means that your Super Self-Love can definitely use a boost.

In my past, every time a relationship ended, no matter who instigated the ending, I started attacking myself. The first line of attack after my breakup with Mr. X was the internal scream: "You are broken!" This stemmed from my belief that water seeks its own level; the fact that I drew in a broken guy meant that I was broken.

I felt like a broken china teacup held together with El-mer's glue, bound to fall apart again. The kind of glue you use is key, though, and Super Self-Love is the ultimate glue. If we try to put ourselves together with a new romance—or anything sourced from outside ourselves—we are bound to break again. Slowly, over the course of the year after this breakup, I discovered that I needed to love myself in order to put myself back together, good as new. I don't expect my cup will ever be shattered again, because I can't imagine any life event that could truly unglue me. I now know that Super Self-Love is the superglue I can dip into whenever necessary.

Before I entered superhero training camp, there were many pieces of myself that I didn't love—or even like, for that matter. I never wanted to sit with the angry or sad Bridget. But I realized I wasn't really going to heal all the layers of my wounded heart if I didn't let myself feel it all fully—the good, the bad, and the ugly. It was during this time that I noticed I welcomed silence in my life. I wanted the house quiet—no more television comedies, less time on the phone. No more need to distract myself with being busy.

One day, after discovering this newfound peace, I received the news that my friend's dog, Toby, had terminal cancer. Instead of distracting myself, I let myself be really sad. There is something about animals suffering that has always leveled me. I can't even go to Disney movies—even the animated ones—because some animal always dies. The suffering of animals is akin to the suffering of children for me. The innocence. It's just too much. I offered to have Toby stay with me and my dogs during the days when my friend was at work. I had to let myself really dive into those sad feelings to be strong enough to make that offer. I was so sad to lose our buddy. His loss touched the piece of my heart where every other pet I had ever lost was resting. Nurturing him over those last weeks of his life gave me space to grieve. It let me practice exposing the sad parts of my heart.

Loving the sad and mad parts of me has been crucial to my developing Super Self-Love. And yet, our feelings are not the be-all and end-all that should guide us. Feelings can be very wise and valuable guides, but they can bring us to a potential source of kryptonite. Up to this point, I have encouraged you to honor your feelings as guideposts on your healing path—particularly when you are very raw at the beginning of your healing. You need to take care of those feelings in order to get to the source of the shadows that may be speaking through them. They are the cookie crumbs leading you on the path to becoming Love Strong.

But there is kryptonite hiding in those feelings when we become wedded to the stories that created them. We can fall in love with the repetition of these stories, so the trigger for the feelings never goes away.

Feelings are meant to be like clouds. You can't lock them in a box to keep them the same shape and size forever. It's important to leave your heart open to a slight breeze so you can process those feelings and let them move through you. Sometimes they will naturally diffuse. Sometimes distractions will take you away from them. Someone calls and changes your state of mind; a piece of cake pushes down the feelings; a situation changes for the better; a wounded child distracts you from your own internal aches; a TV sitcom takes you away ever so briefly from your own "sitdram." Whatever force shifts the feelings, the truth is that feelings can and do transform.

Yet many of us build invisible altars to our feelings, where we try to capture our almighty fleeting emotions and honor them. We cater to them, light candles for them, and put a pretty, soft cloth under them. "Oh, you beautiful feelings, please let me honor you. Let me feed you something delicious to show you that I love you. Mwah!" This makes us feel as if we are honoring ourselves, or even as if we are loving ourselves. But these altars can keep us stuck. They also don't acknowledge the ever-transforming nature of a feeling.

These altars affect your behavior as you protect and honor your feelings instead of dealing with them. Then your behavior affects the offerings you place on that altar. I have a tendency to overeat when I ignore my feelings. If I don't manage them, I eat the feelings. The altar gets more ornate, and the meals I place on it become more fattening and sugary. When I pretend that I don't have the feelings, the altar grows even more lavish. But the simple act of addressing the feelings takes away their need for an altar.

In relationships, we often silently and tacitly tend to our own invisible altars. From time to time, we drag each other over to them and point out how important, big, and grand our own feelings are.

Look at this! Do you see how big that need is? If you don't honor it, I don't know what I'll be forced to do.

In front of my feelings altar, I can be found saying: "Yes, Bridget, your feelings matter more than anything. So if you *feel* like doing something, well then, gosh darn it all, you just go ahead and do it. Because your feelings are the most important thing in the whole wide world."

Super Self-Love empowers you to listen to your feelings, learn from them, and then let them flow—like the Bellamy Brothers song *Let Your Love Flow.* This superpower is the most delicious and nutritious sustenance for your Mighty Flame.

The mantra for this superpower is:

Love flows in and out of my heart with ease.

The following exercise is a particularly good one if you find yourself saying things like: "But, you don't understand my situation. My feelings about this are important, valid, and solid because of these reasons." I get you. I really get you. I am you. But this exercise will clear any feelings altar you may have built that is blocking your Super Self-Love.

Love Strong Exercise: The Feelings Altar

Find a box, jar, vase, or bowl that you love but aren't currently using. This will be the vessel that will safely hold and protect all the feelings you give it.

Name the strong feelings you have—the ones that feel as if they are holding you in a grip so tight you can barely breathe. Maybe you are feeling frustration, anger, sadness, or fear. Whatever your feelings, jot them down on individual pieces of paper and throw them into the vessel.

Make a beautiful feelings altar in a private, yet accessible corner of your bedroom or home where you can keep this little vessel. Lay a nice cloth or handkerchief underneath it and perhaps place a fresh flower in a small vase and a candle beside it. Whenever those big feelings surface, write them down and toss them into the vessel.

Pick a date in the future, a few weeks or more out. Mark it on your calendar. This will be your "open sesame" date—the date on which you will read all the feelings you have put on the altar. Until that day, whenever you have feelings that make you seem less than powerful, write them down (even if it's the same one each day), and place them on your feelings altar. No feeling or need is too trivial. This altar is powerful. It can hold it all. Here are some examples:

- I'm mad because I haven't had time for myself in weeks.
- I still miss my mom.
- I'm pissed that Amy won't call me back.
- I wish I could afford a massage.
- I feel invisible.
- I resent that I'm not treated fairly at work.
- I feel like a loser.
- I just want someone to love me.

When your "open sesame" date arrives, set aside some un-interrupted quiet time to look at all your feelings. Notice which ones have completely disappeared, although you may have assumed they would never go away. Notice the themes. Are you always the hero? Always the victim? Never respected? Always the caretaker? If you have some persistent complaints, start looking in your heart for the shadows that are begging for your attention. There may be something stopping you from getting what you need or want.

Most important, notice that most of these feelings came and went like clouds in the sky pushed by the winds. Your Mighty Flame wants these feelings to move along and helps push them on their way. The more Love Strong you become, the more quickly you will be able to release them.

If this helped you, you may be ready to take your altar down. Or you may want to keep it up for another round or two until you feel confident that your feelings really will keep moving along if you let them.

SUPER ALIGNMENT

When you are super-aligned, you know who you are, what you stand for, and who and what your highest self is drawn to and desires. You don't question your heart; you do its bidding and live from its truth. This is the superpower that most directly fuels your Mighty Flame. It burns bright when you are acting in alignment with your beliefs and passions. It surges when inspired by divine forces.

We have all done things we know are not in our best interest, about which we have a gut instinct telling us to run in the opposite direction. I have many friends, including myself, who have tried to please the dating gods—or the Great Bestower of Lovers from Above—by dismissing the truth about what attracts them. One friend told me he has never been attracted to a certain body type, so he thought he should push himself to engage with that type, as if it were a form of penance that would return great benefits. Stretching yourself is great, but to push yourself past your inner knowing is to step away from your Super Alignment.

Our attractions are usually indications of what can light us up, what ultimately feeds our Mighty Flame. However, if we are attracted to dysfunctional people or situations, then we've got an issue. If you equate violence with love, for instance, you have some work to do to extricate yourself from that pattern. Your most divine self would never draw you toward pain or suffering. The more Super Alignment you have, the clearer the signals that lead you toward that which builds the flame will be.

We also need to keep our fears in check and make sure that we are not using them to stymie our truth, but rather to expand our connection to it. In my friend's case, he feared he wouldn't find someone to whom he was naturally attracted, so he tried to expand his realm of attraction. From the outside looking in, I could see that fear was guiding him. I also could see his construct of a punishing God whom he thought might be pleased with some personal suffering.

When speaking about a boyfriend who wasn't treating her with respect, one girlfriend said: "I think this may be as good as it gets." I promised her that the man who belittled her routinely in front of others and who told her she would never find anyone who loved her more, was not as good as it could get. She admitted she was afraid of being alone. It was, indeed, as good as it *would* get until she dealt with the fear of being alone.

When you are super-aligned, fear doesn't stop you in your tracks because you trust that you will know what to do—even when you are in danger. When the true villain that Wonder Woman must defeat is suddenly revealed, she must instantly let go of her preconceptions and call on all of her powers to destroy him. She is crystal clear in her mission because her Super Alignment is strong. She sees the truth, knows the truth, and her power rises through it. At that moment in time, her connection to the Divine is heightened. When you are super-aligned, you are fortified by the Divine and you don't have to shift your truth for anyone or anything else.

Sometimes, on the other hand, we can be really good at creating fear where none is warranted. I used to live in a fairly secluded area, surrounded by very quiet neighbors whose homes were distanced from my own. There was a wide belt of quiet green space around me. When I first moved in, I was scared at night. I loved the quiet expanse during the day, but at night, I was terrified by all the dark shadowy places and the trees and bushes that obscured my view of any possible imminent danger. I imagined burglars and murderers lurking just beyond the shrubs.

For the first week I lived there, I was scared to be out in my backyard alone in the dark—even with my dogs. Then I started to familiarize myself with my space. I learned about the neighbors (not serial killers, it turns out!) and checked out what was beyond my immediate view. The unknown became known and I began to feel completely safe.

Someone once said to me: "The scariest neighborhood is the one between your two ears." My new backyard was, in fact, not at all scary. But the chatter inside my head was terrifying. When you are super-aligned, you indulge in less fearmongering mental chatter and enjoy more trust. Super-heroes always feel safe no matter what the circumstance. Even in the face of danger, they have a knowledge deep inside that guides them through the fear.

When you are super-aligned, you are equipped to handle anything that comes your way. You also end up being a champion for the Super Alignment of others. When you are aligned, you can't help but be your highest self. One way to determine how super-aligned you are is to ask yourself: "Who am I *being?*" Are you being kind and loving? Remember, we are human *be*ings who feel and think and act out of our being-ness. Everything springs forth from that being-ness. If you are on edge and aggravated, your words and actions (even the way you drive) are all affected. If you are filled to the brim with love, your thoughts and behavior will reflect that. When your thoughts and actions come from a love for yourself and others, you have achieved Super Alignment.

While navigating the landscape of my breakup with Mr. X, I had to ask myself a lot of questions about who I was *being* at that time:

- What did I gain by being in a relationship with a liar?
- What characteristics does a person who tolerates liars have?
- What parts of my life are easier for me when I am with a liar?
- What doesn't work in my life when I am with a liar?
- What is the impact on my friends and family when I am with a liar?

Answering all of these questions pointed me straight back to my own fears. I was afraid of the truth in all its many forms. The biggest truth I was avoiding was that I didn't love myself as much as I thought I did. It was a rude awakening.

So, who was I *being?* I was:

- Someone who was not true to myself, because I didn't value myself as much as I thought he valued me.
- Someone who didn't value my light, my spirit, my truth.
- Someone who couldn't say "I love you" to myself in as shiny and sparkly a way as he said it to me.
- Someone who sometimes ignored my gut instincts when in a relationship.

What does that all add up to? I was dodging the truth—the truth of who he was, the truth of what our relationship was, the truth of how present I was, and the truth of how scared I was. I had rose-colored glasses so firmly affixed to my face that I couldn't even peek over the top of them. I twisted myself into a pretzel to make sense of his lies. I claimed I wanted a deep intimate relationship, but how much intimacy can you have when you choose a liar?

When you have Super Alignment, you live your truth. You can rip off the rose-colored glasses and look the truth right in the eyes. You feel buoyed up, able to make deep dives into the dark seas, knowing you will pop up again and be in the light. For true intimacy, you have to know you can dive into the dark and feel supported and loved no matter what. A loving partner or dear friend can give you this support, but the one person who can do that time and again is the one you see in the mirror. You have the power inside you to do this right now.

Super Alignment is an inside job. A new pair of shoes won't help you with this power—even the most kick-ass shoes on earth. It's the one thing that you and only you know for yourself, the one thing no one can touch. You are divine. As you are. Right now. You are a divine being.

If you haven't ever felt a connection to something divine—a force bigger than yourself, outside of you or inside of you—it's a connection worth making. A sense of wonder and awe feeds your Mighty Flame and helps you to step into your superhero self. Here are some things that may help you hear the whisper of the Divine in you:

- Go out in nature and just let the beauty in, imagining that beauty is actually a force that can reach out and ever so gently touch your heart.
- Pay attention to synchronicities in your life, the uncanny magical timings or mishaps that lead you to a perfect place at the perfect time to see someone or something you might otherwise have missed.
- Think back to childhood memories of playing or exploring alone—times when you felt buoyed up by a force greater than yourself that came from inside you, perhaps a perception that all was perfect no matter what.
- Play music that makes you feel love, loved, or loving. Your heart is your divinity barometer. A guitar solo, a single note, or a drum beat—whatever sends you to a place of perfection warrants your focus.
- Go to holy places and check in with the energy of the millions of humans who have come to these places to connect to the Divine—even if it has nothing to do with your own faith. Just listen for the love and prayer still floating in the air.

Super Alignment is the superpower that grows in strength with stillness and turning inward. Meditation is the tool that helps me align, but I have been experiencing and practicing my connection with the Divine for a long time. The more you rest in that place, or seek experiences that take you there, the more easily you can dip into it when you really need an anchor. Do I still have issues feeling that Super Alignment when I am scared or super-stressed? Absolutely! Sometimes I practically have to throw myself down to meditate! But the bottom line is that the more I meditate, the more super-aligned I am.

One full moon, after a particularly exhausting work week, I was chanting and meditating in front of my outdoor fire pit. The fire was powerful, the flames dancing in a most playful way. I watched the fire until it had nearly died out. I went to bed and meditated even more before I fell asleep. When I woke up the next day, I felt as if my internal fuel tank had been completely filled. I was peaceful and yet full of energy. I went out to do my morning meditation near the fire pit. As soon as I sat down, a hummingbird came to dance around my head. It sat on a tree branch right above me and chirped (I didn't even know hummingbirds could chirp), letting me know it was there, and yet staying far enough away so as not to distract. When I was done with the meditation, it flew circles around me to let me know it was still with me. When you enjoy Super Alignment, magical things like this happen with more and more regularity. I remain in awe of these signs and little synchronicities, while I also now take responsibility for *being* the energy that draws them toward me.

Our state of being can draw love, compassion, and empathy toward us and push anger, resentment, and judgment away. I wondered how many mornings the little hummingbird had been fluttering around me before I ever noticed it. Later that same day, I saw a sign for a moving sale. I was going to be late for an appointment and didn't have much time, but I wanted to see if there was anything of interest I could snag for a bargain price. I walked in and right at the entrance was a shelf I had been imagining for the sliver of real estate right next to my desk. It was the exact wood color, height, and width I had pictured and had the number of shelves I needed. I had thought only days prior: "Well, the only thing that could fit there would be . . ." And there it was!

Then I got a little cocky. I said to myself: "Well, the only other thing I need is lounge chairs for the garden so I can sit and write comfortably on my laptop or recline to have a nice relaxing nap." As I paid for the shelf, the woman asked: "Hey, would you be interested in those garden chairs?" She pointed off in the distance to two beautiful, vintage metal chairs. I had seen them when I first arrived but didn't give them even a fleeting thought because they were far too cool to be for sale and were in an area that was marked as off-limits.

Honestly, God? Instant manifestation? How can this be?

I sat down in one and pushed back. Yes, they reclined! I couldn't believe how perfect they would be for both working and lounging in my garden. I asked how much they were, expecting them to be a lot. They were a steal—a garden-filling writing-enhancing bargain!

This is how miracles happen when you enjoy Super Alignment.

Prayer is another way to get super-aligned. I have meditated for a long time, but I had always had a bit of an odd relationship with prayer. I thought it was something religious people did, and it sounded somehow selfish and less democratic to those of us who were not religious folks.

Do people who know how to pray get dibs on God's blessings?

Then the breakup with Mr. X led me to a very powerful relationship with prayer. My friend Salle Redfield recommended the Prayer of Saint Theresa to ease the fire in my heart. I soon understood exactly why she suggested it. It felt like a prescription, both in its delivery and its receipt. It was a true salve. I printed it up on a little piece of paper that I kept with me at the beginning of my journey. I also kept a copy next to my bed and read it first thing in the morning and last thing at night when I was in the throes of heart pain.

May today there be peace within.
May I trust God that I am exactly
    where I am meant to be.
May I not forget the infinite possibilities
    that are born of faith.
May I use these gifts that I have received,

and pass on the love that has been given to me.
May I be content knowing I am a child of God.
Let this presence settle into my bones,
and allow my soul the freedom to
   sing, dance, praise, and love.
It is there for each and every one of us.

This single prayer changed my relationship with prayer forever. I finally understood why so many people found comfort in it. Reading those lines made me feel immediately nurtured. Praying now feels like a direct line to God. It puts my heart in some sort of good and right order, focused on something far bigger than myself. I am humbled and connected to my own little divining rod.

Desperate times call for desperate measures. At the beginning of this process, I put affirmations all over my house to remind me of a few truths and to help me stay in Super Alignment. Everywhere I looked, I saw them. They were constant reminders of the truth. They helped me remember who I was underneath the pain when I needed a reminder. I did this for the first fiery weeks and then, one day, I knew I didn't need them anymore and I took them all down. I knew that I had internalized them, that I had taken them in on a cellular level.

There was one in particular that I received from Kathy, my very first Love Leaguer, which I put up all over the house. It made a difference at the beginning to keep me in Super Alignment:

I planned it
just
like
this.

Just six little words, but oh so powerful.

I've got this. This is all in my master plan for having a great life. Not sure how this will turn out, but I know I've got this!

Looking back on my time with Mr. X, I realize that my Superhero of Love was trying to get my attention and show me that my Super Alignment was off. Every time he lied, I had an unsettled feeling in my stomach—similar to the feeling I get when I spend money I don't have. I get a little high from the escape from reality, and then, moments later, I am left with my truth: I cannot afford that.

You must be the guardian of your own truth—sometimes even protecting yourself from yourself. When you are super-aligned, you naturally fall into integrity with what's around and inside you. You become the keeper of your Mighty Flame.

The mantra for this superpower to help you stay on track is:

**My life supports my connection
to the Divine.**

The next exercise will help you discover any barriers between you and that connection. If you open a door in your heart to the Divine, you invite that connection to deepen. This exercise will help you identify what may be keeping that door closed tight.

Love Strong Exercise: The Door

Imagine you are standing in front of a set of large, magnificent doors. Take a moment to imagine them in your mind's eye. Perhaps they are carved of wood. Perhaps they are painted a vibrant color. Or maybe they are solid gold or bejeweled. Look at the doors from a comfortable distance, so that you can see them in their entirety. Each door has an exquisite handle. Imagine all the details and even how the handle would feel in your hands.

Your inner knowing tells you what is on the other side of the doors: the road to Super Alignment.

Now, ask yourself the following questions and write the answers as fast as you can—lightning fast! Don't think. Just write. Even if it feels wrong, just write!

- Can I declare that the space behind these doors is "safe"?
- Is there anything on the other side that frightens me?
- Is there anything on the other side that excites me?
- What's the first thing I know I'll feel if I open these doors?
- Is there a specific person or memory of a person—or even a bunch of people—behind the doors?
- Can I allow the doors to open now?

If you are not granted access, don't worry; you can come back! If you are granted access, picture yourself opening the doors with ease and walking through to the other side where the path to Super Alignment awaits you.

Take in what you see in your mind's eye. Before you venture down the path, look ahead and ask yourself these questions:

- Is anything standing between me and Super Alignment?
- Can I gain power over that?
- What actions can I take to overcome the obstacles?
- Who can I ask for help?
- What will Super Alignment look like for me and my life?

You can also have a friend guide you through this process and ask you the questions.

Again, if you are not granted access the first time, don't worry. You may have to come back a couple of times to get to the other side of the doors. Take all the time you need. This is your very own, safe process.

USING YOUR SUPERPOWERS

You now have five superpowers that you can continue to hone. I hope that, at the very least, you are aware that you have always had them. You always had the bravery it takes to look at saboteurs with your Super Sight. You always had the ability to hear the messages of your highest truth with your Super Hearing. You have always bowed in your very own way to greatness with Super Humility. You have always doled out Super Self-Love for yourself in all its many forms. You have, indeed, always had the internal compass of your Super Alignment.

You've had them all along, but working with and using all five superpowers will allow you to give and receive love like never before in your life. Once you become aware of your Mighty Flame, you will likely be inspired to fly—toward love and toward those who need love.

If you need a spark to re-center yourself, use the affirmation reminders in the chart on page 181. These can be your best allies. You can tape them up on your refrigerator or mirror. You can write each affirmation on a little piece of paper (make as many copies as you want), throw them into a bowl or jar, and grab one just as you would a little snack—only this snack will give your soul a big energy boost!

The Five Superpowers

	Body Part	Symbolizes	Affirmation
SUPER **Sight**	Eyes	Clarity and the ability to see, even in the shadows	*I have the courage to see clearly.*
SUPER **Hearing**	Ears	Connection to your truth and inner guidance	*I hear the wisdom. I hear the love.*
SUPER **Humility**	Feet	Grounding energy and humility	*My heart is open to the touch of seen and unseen magnificence.*
SUPER **Self-Love**	Heart	Giving and receiving	*Love flows in and out of my heart with ease.*
SUPER **Alignment**	Top of the Head	The source of flight	*My life supports my connection to the Divine.*

Feel free to copy this page and keep it somewhere close to remind you of all that your Five Superpowers have to offer you and your Mighty Heart.

Mighty Flame Check-In #3: Final Pre-Flight Check

Are you feeling that Mighty Flame burning bright? Are you starting to know inside and out that you are loved, so very loved? Are you starting to recognize yourself as someone who loves and is loved more and more?

Rate your answers on a scale of 0 to 10, or 10 to 0. I hope you find that you have moved yourself toward the right side of the scale and are feeling that flame, Superhero!

My heart pain level is about:

10   9   8   7   6   5   4   3   2   1   0

My energy level is about:

0   1   2   3   4   5   6   7   8   9   10

My obsessive thinking about my loss is roughly:

10   9   8   7   6   5   4   3   2   1   0

My joy quotient is about:

0   1   2   3   4   5   6   7   8   9   10

Chapter 8

NOW GO SAVE THE WORLD!

*When we employ the energy of love, we are
leaving fear behind us and choosing instead to
make our way toward a new, inspiring goal:
living our lives with open hearts.*
Reverend Ed Bacon, *8 Habits of Love*

Bravo, Superhero! You did it! You stepped into the Temple of
the Mighty Heart, with your heart not even knowing what
it was entering. "What? Superhero? Me?" you may have
screamed. Yet you braved the shadows, honed your superpowers, and turned up the heat on your Mighty Flame. I
hope you assembled a Love League and gathered up some
superhero training coaches. And I hope your heart reveled
in the love and support they gave you.

If you feel as if you may have whipped through this book too quickly, or maybe were confronted along the way with things you didn't really want to face, I encourage you to go back and re-read the parts that made you uncomfortable. You may find that they aren't as difficult as they were before; you may even breeze through them now.

Becoming a Superhero of Love is a process. We are all evolving. But if we stay focused on love, we will firmly entrench ourselves in the realm of a new kind of evolution where love is the answer.

Here are some things you may find true now that you've come this far:

- You allow yourself and others to have their feelings, knowing these are not set in stone.
- You are triggered less by others' emotional responses.
- You have less and less need to protect yourself or others emotionally.
- You find yourself smiling more, scowling less.
- You more readily respond with love.
- People tend to open up and feel at ease around you.
- There's a lot less defending of positions going on in your world.
- At the end of a day by yourself, you remark what a great time you had.
- When people speak of the future, holidays, or trips, you can imagine yourself in that future alone or with a partner—and you are excited by either possibility.

- Less of your day is spent pointing out things that are wrong with people, the world, or your life.
- When you look in the mirror, you find that the negative mantras have decreased.
- You less often find yourself saying: "When X, Y, and/or Z happens, I will be happy."
- You find yourself remarking on things you love about your life a lot more.
- Your joy factor has gone up.
- You feel "filled up" on a regular basis.

Even if you find only a few of these to be true, you can be proud to have achieved them, proud to be on this path. The world needs as many people who embody these traits as possible. The world needs superheroes, so the fact that you even opened up to this book puts you on a direct path to making this world a better place.

While love alone can do a world of good, we will need more than love to heal the world. We need to *stand up* for love and be love warriors. We need to take our convictions outside ourselves, outside our four walls, and into the world. We need to turn up the fire on our Mighty Flames and be like our comic book superhero compatriots—*unstoppable.*

Another important action is to share your Superhero of Love stories. When you tell even one person a story that may spark his or her Mighty Flame, you make a difference in the world. We have all shared ourselves in a way that touched others' hearts. Now that you are a Superhero of

Love, I challenge you to see this as a holy act—an act that adds your story to the Temple of the Mighty Heart.

What if one story you share causes someone to look at a pained relationship with a different eye? What if one story causes people to see themselves as more lovable, more valued, more deserving? What if one story causes them to feel a reawakening of a part of their heart that had been shut down for years?

If you share your story of how you unveiled a saboteur with someone who has never heard of shadow work, what a gift that will be. When you don't know what you don't know, the only thing you can hope for is that someone will come along and gently remove your blinders. I started this work when my friend Fran shared her story about a shadow she had unveiled that was keeping her trapped in negative patterns. Her sharing one story opened up a whole new world for me. Be generous in spreading the word about your mission in the world! Remind friends and family that they have a superhero inside them as well. Here's one I heard on NPR that has been an amazing source of inspiration to me:

Rabbi Michael Weisser, now retired from the Free Synagogue of Flushing, New York, and his wife became caregivers for a man whom no one would have ever guessed would end up in their loving care. Larry Trapp, a Grand Dragon in the Ku Klux Klan, had threatened the rabbi and his family repeatedly upon their arrival in Lincoln, Nebraska, where they had been assigned to a synagogue.

Even though people warned the rabbi that his actions might incite Trapp, the rabbi called Trapp every Thursday afternoon at the same time and left what he called "love messages" on Trapp's answering machine. After some months, Trapp finally returned the rabbi's call, and ultimately asked for his help. Trapp wanted to give up his racist and anti-Semitic beliefs. The Superhero of Love Rabbi had won his battle with the sword of love.

Trapp struggled with diabetes and lost two legs to the disease. In the course of this transformative friendship, he moved into the Weissers' home, where the rabbi's wife cared for him for the last nine months of his life. Prior to his death, he spoke against racism in schools and did great community work to help others like himself. He was just lucky to have found the kind of love he could receive and be healed by before he died. The rabbi and his wife were truly Superheroes of Love.

Superheroes never know when or where they will be called on, or how long it will take to get a job done. That's why we need to hone our skills constantly, so that anything that might block the flow of love is removed. If we can do this for ourselves, then we will be able to take a stand for others, helping them to do the same. The simple act of spreading the word about another Superhero of Love's deed can do a world of good for every heart that hears it. By telling our stories, we stand up for love.

At the beginning of this book, I shared the vision I had of myself as burned into a pile of ash. I also described the vision I had of the future me—the Superhero of Love version of me, my higher, mightier self. She was the one who first led me to the Temple of the Mighty Heart to begin this journey in earnest. When I felt as if I would be consumed by crazy firestorms, it was up to me to find her again. I knew there was only one place to look: inside. Everything I did helped me achieve that—finding my coaches, establishing my Love League, doing the Love Strong Exercises—every little effort drew me closer and closer to that person, until I finally became her.

Tapping into the wisdom and power of past superheroes helped me better imagine myself as one. Imagining myself in the Temple of the Mighty Heart helped me feel the presence of the Divine; it helped me be filled up with love and more connected to God than ever before.

Now I imagine my return late one summer evening to the Temple of the Mighty Heart high atop that hill, feeling so close to the cool full moon above. I am alone again, just as I was at the beginning of my journey, experiencing the power of this holy place without distraction. Crickets are singing. From a nearby tree, an owl tells me he is watching over me. I sit cross-legged, as I have for many months every single day, ready for meditation and messages. I am completely at peace and receive the message I have heard all these many moons since: "I am loved. I am loved. I am loved." And then I hear the whispers, as if thousands are gently reminding me with the sweetest tenderness: "You are loved. You are loved. You are so very loved."

I feel the presence of my dad. I feel the presence of all the wise ones who have brought me to this place. I feel the Superheroes of Love who have come before me—the guides, masters, angels, and teachers I have met in meditations and in body that have buoyed me up, woken me up, brought me back to life, and placed me ever so gently back at this divine spot. I am encircled by loving spirits, both here and in the beyond, whom I recognize have helped me along this journey.

It took a village.

I feel a warm and gentle hand on my back and I hear the words: "Look up." My Superhero of Love is at my side. The presence that first helped me re-form myself—that was there for me through all the firestorms and that is always with me now—points toward a nearby hill just as the most magnificent display of fireworks begins. The glorious acknowledgment of all the work we have done on our hearts lights up the sky, a remembrance of all the love we have conjured anew.

My Superhero of Love wasn't something to aspire to; she was just waiting to be seen, heard, and known. My Superhero of Love wasn't born to help me heal from this breakup. She has been with me every moment of this life, whispering in my ear, holding my hand when I was in despair, reminding me I was loved, connecting and reconnecting me to the Divine every time I doubted or my faith dimmed even slightly. She will be with me on my next journey as well, reminding me:

I am Love Strong.
My Mighty Flame burns bright.

I don't run from saboteurs or kryptonite; I embrace
them and the gifts they hold.
I am inspired to touch other hearts wherever I go.
I will trip over kryptonite; I will fall under the weight
of a saboteur.
And still, I am Love Strong.

And you, dear reader, I hope with all my heart that you feel Love Strong as well. I hope your flame burns bright and that you fly as high as you wish to go. More than anything, I hope you know that you wield extraordinary powers. Power to heal. Power to move mountains. Power to transform. Powers as magical as any superhero's. I wish you love and adventures, and I wish for the essence of this creed, which is etched into the pillar that holds the Mighty Flame in the Temple of the Mighty Heart, to be nestled gently in your heart forever and ever.

The Superhero of Love's Creed

You are loved.
You are love.
You have a Superhero of Love
Inside you right now.
Yes, you, Superhero.
You are that.
You are loved.
You are love.

Postscript: Love Is a Practice

Love alone will lead you on God's Path.
                                          Master John Douglas

On my superhero journey, I discovered that love is an entry point to God. As I close out this book's final moments, I know this more than ever: When we love, we honor God.

Can you imagine that God loves us for loving? We are so supremely loved, each and every one of us. I have an image of all the glorious gods, angels, and wise ones above smiling upon me when I have spent a day loving as well as I possibly can. I wish I could say that happened every day. It doesn't, but I am far better than I was at the beginning of this journey. I practice every day just as Thich Nhat Hanh suggests: "Love is a practice. Love is truly a practice."*

---

* Melvin McLeod, *Lion's Roar,* "This Is the Buddha's Love: An Interview with Thich Nhat Hanh," March 1, 2006.

All I know is that the more I work on becoming Love Strong, the closer I feel to God and the more I realize that this is literally all that matters. So, fly Superhero, fly, because this is kind of a big deal, this love thing. I believe it's why we are all here, and why we were each born with a Superhero of Love inside.

Mighty Flame Boosters

When your Mighty Flame needs a boost, when you are dealing with a particularly potent dose of kryptonite, the following exercises can help. They start with some heart-pain triage for use when you are dealing with a fresh dose of kryptonite or are trapped in a crazy firestorm. Then you will find exercises that are about less urgent heart matters—practices that nurture and cultivate your Mighty Flame. Finally, you will move on to exercises that will help you *fly* into the world with your Superhero of Love self!

You can also just flip through these pages and trust that you will land on the perfect Mighty Flame booster for this moment. Have fun with these exercises. There is no right or wrong way to do them. If one doesn't make a difference one day, try coming back to it another day. You may find that it is the perfect answer to your superhero prayers.

Shake that Etch-a-Sketch

An Etch-a-Sketch is a toy that allows you to create intricate drawings on a screen by turning little knobs left and right. The drawings can take a long time to complete. But if you drop it, or accidentally turn or shake the screen, you can instantly erase all your fine work. It's sort of like the intricate mandalas Tibetan monks create with sand over the course of days or weeks that they then destroy with one stroke of a stick after the complex piece of art is complete. It's good to realize how easy it can be to shift from creation to destruction, from anger to peace, from judgment to an open heart.

- Set a timer for five minutes.
- Choose a person with whom you have a problematic relationship.
- Write down all the harmful things this person has said or done to you. Write as fast as you can to keep your brain and heart firing with the intention of getting as much down as you possibly can. If you go over five minutes, that's fine; just stay focused for at least five minutes on making this list as juicy and full as possible.
- Write down all the harmful things you have done to this person—in word, thought, or deed. Write as fast as you can to keep your brain and heart firing with the intention of getting as much down as you possibly can. If you go over five minutes, that's fine.

When the lists are complete, set them down on an open space on the floor, or even outside if you can remain undisturbed. Look down at the papers and ask yourself if you are willing to step away from them and forgive *both of you* for your trespasses against each other.

If you are willing, stay conscious of your surroundings and take a step back. Then ask yourself again: "Am I willing to step away from this complaint and forgive?"

The act of stepping away from this problematic relationship presented as words on paper can jostle your heart into a new perspective and possibly open it up to new possibilities.

If each step gives you some relief, or at least some pause in the cycle of anger or sadness, then consider repeating the exercise until you are willing to forgive yourself and this person.

Building Core Strength with the Triple A

You need "core" strength to ride the emotional waves after a loss. Contemplating the three words given on page 196 will build core strength by keeping you as present as possible—conscious of the waves, aware of the weather, committed to staying centered, and upright in mind and spirit. Try on each word as you might try on a sweater, and stay conscious of how each one can steady you just by contemplating it.

- Allow: Allowing negative thoughts and feelings to wash over you takes some effort. This was the hardest task for me. But with constant reminders, I finally got the knack of it. The more I labeled my negative feelings as bad or wrong, the longer they hung on and the worse I felt.
- Accept: You are here. You won't be here forever. You are just here now. Again, not easy. I get it. But try it, one moment at a time, until you can string together a lot of moments. Before you know it, you will have moved to another level of healing and power.
- Adapt: It's a new life you have to navigate after a breakup. Imagine yourself as a ninja, moving left and right, up and down with ease, leaping high into the air to avoid quicksand, jumping from tree to tree like a monkey to stay above the crazy firestorms. There's a new normal now. But soon there will be an even newer normal that you create for yourself.

Fairy-Tale Anger Release

If you are currently feeling angry, this exercise may bring you relief. Hold my hand, and let's jump into that possibility.

Think of the person with whom you are angry. Think of why you are angry. Now, imagine you have been transported to stand in front of that person at a moment when you are in the middle of a heated conflict. You are yelling all the things you have wanted to yell and perhaps have held back until now. You are saying it all, giving it your all. The intensity of the argument reaches a crescendo, at which point—stay with me—you are miraculously plucked out of the conflict and swiftly flown far away. You are gently released onto the softest, most comfortable raft imaginable that is floating slowly, calmly down a majestic river.

A gentle voice sweetly announces that this is a magical river that can transmute anger. The calming voice seems to put you quickly to sleep. While you rest, the magic transpires. The anger dissipates. You awaken to a world where understanding and love prevail. For the first time, you understand the other person's position. You turn and see that person floating on another raft. You look into each other's eyes and you see that person now understands your position. You know it. You both feel completely understood.

You understand that you are both just doing your very best in this world.

Imagine that a wise voice returns and whispers in your ear:

Smile like the happy baby
whose anger flows through him
like water flowing over river rock—
angry one moment, happy the next,
happy now, happy now.
Now, choose to be that happy baby.

Imagine the emotions flowing through you, around you. Imagine that, by letting go, by transmuting those stuck feelings, you can remove blocks and open a new flow in the relationship. Our positions are based on our thoughts, triggered by our feelings, and vice versa. The beginning of a transformation can be as simple as allowing yourself to imagine the other side of the conflict.

You can be a magical wizard in your own life. The ability to transmute anger is in your bag of tricks, Superhero. And if you didn't feel that this exercise made a difference today, come back to it another day.

The Forgiving Circle

Imagine that you are in a most beautiful place that makes you happy. Look around for a perfect spot to alight and relax. You are comfortable, the temperature is perfect, the air is fresh.

Check in with your Mighty Flame.

Now, think of someone you have judged and/or who has judged you. Check in with that flame again.

Imagine that person has a spot just like yours and is sitting opposite you. Look into the other person's eyes and say these two things:

- I forgive you for _____. (Allow the person to receive your forgiveness.)
- I wish your forgiveness for _____. (Allow the person to forgive you. Receive that forgiveness.)

Now it's the other person's turn to say these things to you:

- I forgive you for _____. (Allow the person to forgive you. Receive that forgiveness.)
- I wish your forgiveness for _____. (Give the person your forgiveness.)

How does it feel to give and receive forgiveness? Check in one more time with your Mighty Flame.

If you wish, invite another person for whom you have held some anger and resentment to come sit opposite you. Stay in this magical spot as long as you wish.

The Judging Heart

Lie down or sit somewhere comfortably and relax. Pay attention to your body. How do your shoulders, stomach, hands, forehead feel?

Now, think of someone you have been judging. Go over some of your most judgmental thoughts until you are fully enveloped in them: "He is an awful person because . . .";
"She doesn't deserve my love because . . ." Pay attention to your body, where you are tense, etc. Can you name the spot where your judgment resides? Where is it?

Hold on to that tension for another moment, then exhale and let it go, imagining the judgment leaving with the tension.

Now imagine someone for whom you feel great love. Let those loving thoughts fill your heart: "I love him so much because . . ."; "I appreciate her so much." How does your body feel? Where in your body do you feel the love the most? Where in your body does it originate?

Notice the difference in how your body feels in both cases. With this increased awareness of your body and its reaction to judgment and love, when you find yourself judging take a moment to shift your attention to the place where you feel love. Imagine a giant sun is placed in that spot, warming and energizing your efforts and giving you the strength to choose love.

Compassion Builders

The payoff for growing your compassion quotient is huge. It will expand and strengthen your heart. It will grow your Mighty Flame and juice up all your superpowers. But you have to look at what is blocking your compassion before you can cultivate it. Here are three techniques that can help you do just that:

- Compassion Builder #1: Shadows can be brutal; they completely lack compassion. One of my shadows thinks feelings are a waste of time. She would like us all to leave our feelings tucked away in the darkest of corners. She was born when I was five years old and started making my own lunches—when I realized I needed to step up and parent myself, and be as perfect a kid as I could be. She's a bitchy-witchy one who thinks stopping for feelings is a sign of weakness—dare I say, failure.

- Think of a time when you couldn't muster compassion for someone else. Perhaps others around you could easily feel this person's pain, but you had very good reasons why you could not. Now imagine that the judgmental voice inside you has a form, a face, a voice, and a name. Giving that shadow a form and identity will help you converse with her in the future. I have to talk to my shadow, tell her that I've got her back, and help hold her aching heart.

- Compassion Builder #2: Sometimes we really can't see another's point of view because we have never felt their pain. We have to soften our own hearts and dive into theirs. This can happen in one simple conversation in which we share each other's pain, hold that pain for a little while, and be supportive and loving.

  - Think of someone you are judging right now, perhaps your Mr. X. Think of three circumstances, past or present, that made him who he is, and imagine what it would be like if you had been in his shoes. List three feelings you might have if you were him. Think of the lenses through which you might look at the world. Think of the chips you might have on your shoulder, the natural predilections.

- Compassion Builder #3: We think we don't have the same negative traits that other people have. The good news and the bad news is that, if you can "name" an undesirable quality in another person, you've got a shadow just sitting around waiting to be identified. Owning up to that quality in yourself can provide a window on compassion.
  - Think of a most unsavory characteristic that you judge harshly in others. Bring to mind someone who has this characteristic and spend a few minutes mulling over why you dislike this characteristic. Identify the behavior it causes, and the effects it has on others. Then stop and clear the slate in your mind as best as you can. Now, look inside and see where that characteristic, or a version of it, lives in you. For instance, I may not have been a liar on the same scale as my Mr. X, but I can see where I am not truthful to myself or others because I sometimes don't want to dig too deeply or be truly seen.

Allowing and Accepting

Think of the last time you pulled back from someone's anger or sadness, wishing you could escape those emotions. Perhaps you actually did retreat, or maybe you just felt as if you couldn't deal with it.

Now, let's rewrite that scene. Imagine yourself back in that moment. Imagine the person is expressing those emotions, letting out all the sadness or anger he or she has—all of it, even all the reserves. Nothing left. The person takes a breath and looks at you. You take a breath and look back for a moment—then you give that person the biggest warmest hug, one that conveys your pure love and acceptance.

You may not be in a place to do this the next time someone's emotions come rushing out, but your heart may flutter with a new compassion. You may also recognize when someone wants to do it for you.

We have all missed many opportunities to give and receive love. Maybe next time you won't miss out.

Clutter Buster

If you look around your house and find areas of clutter or things you don't like that are ugly or that simply don't make you feel good, clear them out. Physical clutter becomes mental clutter. Any one of the following tasks can give you a boost.

- Clean out a closet.
- Donate all the clothes you haven't worn in more than a year.
- Reorganize a drawer, closet, or room.
- Clean out your cupboards.

- Pay off a credit card.
- Balance your checkbook.
- Send an overdue birthday card.
- Wash your car.
- Clean out the trunk of your car or glove compartment.

Listen Up, Up, Up!

Learning how to listen is ideally a solitary pursuit. You are alone—just you, your breath, and your own little inner monologue. When you sit quietly with your inner chatter, you start to learn how to sift through it.

Listening to birds is one way to do this. Hopefully, you live in a place where you can sit quietly and listen for birds. If not, seek out a nearby park or nature reserve where you can sit—particularly in the early morning or at dusk when birds tend to make their songs heard by all.

Listen for their various calls. Try to distinguish one from the next. What makes them different? When you connect with singular sounds and focus on them, you invite yourself to turn up your Super Hearing.

Single-pointed focus is a superhero power that takes practice. Have fun with it!

These Three Things

Name three things you love about your life. Put your arms up in front of you, as if you are stopping a crowd from coming toward you, and say these words: "Thank you for _____, _____, and _____," filling in the blanks with the three things you just named.

Now put your arms down at your sides, with your palms wide open facing peacefully in front of you, as if they emanate pure unconditional love, and repeat those words again: "Thank you for _____, _____, and _____," again filling in the blanks with the three things you just named.

Do you notice the difference that just the placement of your arms can make to your emotional state? We can lead our hearts to vulnerability by adjusting our body language. This helps a lot when you are in conflict, or your heart is constricted. Notice how you can make conflict recede and your heart soften merely by taking an open stance. As Superheroes of Love, we have so many opportunities to cause these shifts, to seize opportunities to take the vulnerability lead. It only takes one person in a conflict to initiate the softening of the heart that can lead you toward peace.

Suit Up

Imagine there's an outfit crafted especially for you by "The Designer to All Superheroes."

What color is it? What material? Do you have an emblem on your chest? Do you have special shoes? Jewelry? A snazzy belt? A superhero emanates light. Imagine where that superhero light comes from. Is it the same place where your Mighty Flame resides? Does it shine from your eyes? Emanate from your fingers? Or from your third eye? Your chest? Your solar plexus? Do you have a headlamp on your forehead as part of your superhero gear?

Come up with as many details as you can. Let your imagination go wild and then draw or create a collage of images that depict what you have in mind. The more fun you have with this in your mind's eye, the more fun you will have living into the spirit of what you create.

Post the collage or picture where you will see it often so that it can inspire you.

Tea Time

Tea has been a really great tool for me to help develop Super Humility. Even though I always start my day with coffee—another ritual I adore—I have a newfound appreciation for calming tea time. This is a practice that I started specifically to slow myself down and stop the busy-ness that tends to overwhelm me when I am in pain. It helps me to be present in the here and now.

When I am emotionally on fire in crisis mode, I literally have to make myself stop for tea time. Just the act of making tea can start the process of getting present. Sometimes my thoughts wander to whatever is upsetting me, so I refocus on the actions I am performing and engage in a silent running commentary to stay in the moment: "I am putting water in the kettle. I am turning on the kettle." It's like a meditation that provides me with an inner and outer cure to chaos. A calming tea affects your body chemistry and the process calms your body movements and thoughts.

Exploring teas is an adventure and making new friends who have a calming effect on you is always a good idea. If you don't like tea, choose something that makes you stop, slow down, and get present. I know many women who enjoy a glass of red wine or a cocktail in the evening. Just make sure that you are not self-medicating or taking yourself too far away from your feelings on a regular basis. Use whatever floats your boat and allows you to just "be" in the moment.

First Date

My friend Adelaide always says: "Offer friendship first. Then see where it goes." This is also good advice for the friendship we offer ourselves on our journey to Super Self-Love. This exercise is for people who have recently broken up a long-term relationship and are learning to enjoy life on their own again. It's also good for anyone who cringes at the idea of going to a movie or nice restaurant alone, whether in a relationship or not. You are going to take yourself out on a date.

If you particularly dislike being alone in public, perhaps you can start with a movie. Find a movie you are excited to see and pick a time that works for you. How easy is that? No one else's schedule to accommodate! Buy your ticket, and your favorite drink or snack. You don't even have to share your treats!

Try to remain conscious of your feelings and thoughts as you go. If you have anxiety, just watch it, and let it go if you can. When you do different things or do things differently, it's normal to have uncomfortable rumblings in your heart or mind.

At the end of your date, as you return home, notice that you can enjoy your own thoughts about the movie, or sit and tap into your own emotions about it. How does it feel to consider only your own unadulterated opinions and feelings with no one to question you, or even offer an alternate point of view?

When you are done, consider how the date went. Are you interested in a second?

If it isn't love at first sight, don't worry. The healthiest love affairs start slowly—with friendship first, of course.

Love Letter

Write yourself a little love letter to tell yourself how much you appreciate your own company. Be as creative or simple as you wish. Boosting your flame is an inside job.

Example:

Dear Me,

I loved how we took an extra-long dog walk today, because the sunshine felt really nurturing. I loved how we got our work done so we could go to bed early. I loved how we shut off our phone for the afternoon. I love how we booked a time to see girlfriends.

Love,

Me

I Wanna Hold Your Hand

This exercise is so simple that it blew me away when I discovered it. I was reading an article online and was compelled to feel my hands to see if I needed some lotion. I had been gardening all day and realized that, indeed, lotion would be a great idea. But I had come to a riveting part of the article, so I didn't want to stop. Several minutes later, I became aware that I was still holding my own hand. When you put your hand out to shake someone else's, the other person gives you his or her hand, making a connection. In the same way, you can make a connection by clasping your own hand—you are just connecting with yourself. You are making a circle of love.

So hold your own hand. Close your eyes. Feel the flow of energy—hand to heart to hand, hand to heart to hand. What a lovely unending opportunity to give love to yourself.

We can each be our very own ever-replenishing, constant source of love.

Divine Messages

If you have never felt a nudge from the other side—perhaps from someone who has passed away trying to communicate with you—don't worry. This exercise taps into the possibility that you may be able to have a chat with someone you have lost. Pick a person you want to contact at this moment in your superhero journey.

If this feels very far-fetched, try writing a letter expressing how you have felt since the person passed away. This is a good way to get yourself to a heart-centered and open place. Don't judge any thoughts or feelings you may have. It's all perfect.

When you are done, keep your fingers on your keyboard (or pen in your hand) and ask if the person you chose has a response. You may think that you are making it up at first. That's okay, too. Don't judge yourself or the place from where the words are coming. Just let it rip.

When I first started doing this, I tried not to "read" as I typed. I focused on listening to each word as it came through and made myself wait to read the message until it was complete.

Try not to judge anything in the process, including the length of the message, if one comes. And, if nothing comes, just try another day.

If you don't want to write a letter, try asking questions of your beloved. See if you can hear the answers.

Whatever happens is perfect. If you need to set this to the side for now and perhaps come back to it, just earmark the page and try again another day!

Thank You Letters

The word "gratitude" is tossed around a lot these days, especially by those of us in the game of transformation. And there's a good reason for that. Gratitude provides a direct path to boosting your Mighty Flame. You can express gratitude by writing a thank-you letter, or you can even write your thoughts in a journal.

When I start my day with gratitude, it really does give my day a little more sheen. You can wake up and simply say what you are grateful for, or you can grab a journal and write: "Dear God (Spirit, Angels, Source), thank you for my beautiful house, my most perfect two dogs, the flowers in my bedroom . . ."

Try to identify at least three things a day. Don't worry if you repeat things—just be honest.

Try doing this as soon as you wake up or just before going to sleep to make it a nice little ritual that doesn't have to accommodate life's requirements. We always go to bed and we always get up. By tying your gratitude ritual to regular events in your life, you ensure that you will be consistent in your practice.

How about a practice session? How about a little super-hero stretch? Give me ten things you are grateful for right this moment.

Now check in with that flame.

Passion Tap

One way to spark your Mighty Flame is to tap into your passions. Sometimes we lose sight of what used to draw us forward through life before we experienced loss. Here's a way to tap into those sparks with just three little steps.

Make a list of at least five things that have inspired your passion in the past. Some people have to go back to their childhood. Wherever you find these things in your memory bank is perfect.

Make a list of at least five passions that you remember admiring in another. You don't have to see yourself doing that same thing; just tap into the admiration. What about the person's passion did you admire? Was it what it awakened in the heart of that person, or what it took to achieve it?

Look at both lists. Does anything strike you as something you may want to reawaken? Did something new get sparked as you contemplated these passions? Write down what you discovered. You don't have to act on it today, but recording what you discovered is a way of honoring what you found. If something is meant to inspire action, it will—if you honor it and allow it.

Up, Up, and Away!

Here are three questions to ask yourself. They may look similar, but if you ask and answer them very quickly, you will see for yourself how different they are:

- What makes my heart sing?
- What makes me smile?
- What lifts me up?

Then finish one or all of these sentences:

- My life is happier when . . .
- My life is better when . . .
- My life works better when . . .
- My life is lovely when . . .

A Work of HeART

When you have started embodying the love you want to have in your life, I challenge you to write your future love story.

Here are some questions you can ask yourself if you are looking for inspiration:

- How does it begin? Where do you meet?
- What does the other person look like, do, etc.?
- What does he care about?

- How is he with animals? Kids? Wait staff? Customer Service reps?
- How does he like to spend his time alone? How do you like to spend your time alone when you are in a relationship with him?
- What do you love doing together?
- Where do your passions sync up?
- Are you "of service" as a couple? Do you volunteer or give to friends in a way that feels good?
- How do you spend your days? Do you always have dinner together? Do you have weekend adventures? How often do you have sex?

Here are some ways you can start your story:

- Once upon a time . . .
- They met . . .
- I found myself . . .

You can write a fairy tale, a bodice-ripper romance novel, a poem, a short story, a song—whatever you choose. Just start imagining what life could be like. If you don't like working with words, create a collage or a painting. Use whatever medium works for you.

No one needs to see it but you. So, let your imagination carry you away. When you've completed your story—your "work of HeART"—ask yourself these questions:

- Can you envision yourself in this story? The "you" that is sitting in your chair right now or lying in your bed as you read this? You? Can you see yourself living that reality—not an actress playing you, but the honest-to-God, through-and-through super-aligned version of you?
- If not, what do you need to work on, transform, or bring to another level to make it so you can see your real self in that vision?
- Are there any ducks you need to get in a row? Any messes you need to clean up? Debts you want to pay? Weight you want to lose? Sometimes we envision the best version of ourselves in our future stories. That best version of you is there; it just may require some dusting off.
- Do you feel you deserve that love story? Does it make you feel uncomfortable? If yes, maybe there are some things you can do to help you feel deserving.

Now consider: Have you ever had anything close to the love story you wrote? If you have always been in relationships with people who belittled you, and in your vision your love treats you like a queen, the only question to ask is: Have you gotten to the bottom of why you allowed men to treat you differently in the past? You may have it wired, or re-wired, I should say. Excellent, if that is the case. But if you haven't yet done it, venture into the shadows and look at what is there that might stop you from being treated like a Superhero of Love.

Now let it go! Let go of the story of what you want and the vision associated with it—the soundtrack of your future wedding and the credits rolling at the end. Let it all go and . . .

Live. Be happy.

The Five Superpowers

Finally, let's recap the five superpowers, their elements, and their affirmations:

SUPER SIGHT
Elements:

- The ability to shed light into the darkest places so you can see the hidden kryptonite as well as the hidden jewels
- The power to see through the muck, the walls, and the barriers to the unseen, hidden saboteurs yet to be uncovered
- The magic that comes from unveiling all that stops you from seeing love in all its forms

Affirmation:

I have the courage to see clearly.

SUPER HEARING

Elements:

- The ability to hear the truth, your highest truth, your spirit
- The power to hear guidance when it comes from the source, Spirit, God, etc.
- The magic of sifting through the noise for the crystal-clear notes of the truth

Affirmation:

I hear the wisdom. I hear the love.

SUPER HUMILITY

Elements:

- The ability to tap into a force that is greater than yourself
- The power that comes when you see the divinity in others
- The magic that comes from exercising your gratitude muscle

Affirmation:

My heart is open to the touch of seen and unseen magnificence.

SUPER SELF-LOVE

Elements:

- The ability to fall in love with yourself so you can be your forever soul mate
- The power that comes from loving your broken heart back to health
- The magic that comes from giving yourself what you need to feel truly loved

Affirmation:

Love flows in and out of my heart with ease.

SUPER ALIGNMENT

Elements:

- The ability to tap into your highest truth at lightning speed
- The power to transcend that which stands between you and your inner knowing
- The magic of creating anything you wish from that place of oneness

Affirmation:

My life supports my connection to the Divine.

Acknowledgments

It took a village to build this superhero castle—all of them kings and queens to me. I bow to them all.

The first draft was blessed by the eyes of Kate Kelly Raffetto Gallegos, who was also one of the founding members of my Love League. And the very last draft was blessed by Jean Marie Black, whose eye is as sharp as her wicked smart wit. Formative drafts gathered substantial steam under the watchful eye of Carol Woodliff, Leanne Wood, Elisa Bruley (aka owner of Elisa B., the best little dress shop in Old Pasadena mentioned on page 25), Robin Rouse, Pamela Donovan, and Liora Elghanayan, all of whom provided key criticisms and cheerleading to keep me moving forward. Liora wins a special superhero prize, though, as she read nearly every draft in its entirety and somehow was able to bring a fresh eye each time. I bow deeply to Queen Liora.

Tim Blankenhorn, my first writing mentor, proofread a key chapter late one night when I couldn't see straight. (My hero!) Franz Metcalf, the giant-hearted Buddhist scholar and author of many heart-sparking books, was so generous when reading a draft that was far too early for his wise eyes. He didn't make me feel even slightly inadequate for my trespass.

There were others who read bits and pieces along the way: Erin Baer, Alexandra Ballard, and my dear friend who doesn't even like self-help books, Elizabeth Keyishian Wilks. (Now, that's love!) My Facebook posse cheered me on from all over the globe, as did the friends in my own neighborhood, Susan Streets and Carol Chenoweth. I am deeply grateful for every cheerful word of encouragement and each sincere offer to help in any way they could.

Adelaide Hixon and Ann Clothier, PhD, two friends I mention multiple times (by their first names) are guiding lights in my life. They both have an uncanny ability to ground me and inspire me to be a better person. And they both make me laugh really hard. I will forever be beholden to Ann for having written the letter that brought me to Master John Douglas. I am her happy humble servant for this bolt of lightning to my heart and soul.

I once met a woman on an airplane going from Burbank to San Jose who knew someone going through a painful divorce. That brave woman read an early version of the manuscript and said it inspired her to meditate for the first time in her life. I call that a win, and I thank her for making that draft's pains disappear.

And then there's Pat. In college, I acted in a musical that Pat Verducci cowrote and codirected. She's been kicking ass as a screenwriter and writer of all things word-related ever since. I call her a "book doula." She helped me breathe through the sometimes excruciating final reshapings of the book. I have a hard time with criticism, but Pat delivered hers with such tenderness: "I know you are going to hate me, but I really think you have to . . ." She was right. Always.

The last draft, just before the book was sent out to publishers, was blessed by the kick-ass divine CMA Elite team of Lisa O'Neill, Jan Casebolt, Leslie Elkus, and the ever-faithful Liora. They were all loving, hilarious, and generous, no matter how late at night or early in the morning my request for a divine assist appeared on their phones.

Then it made its way to one of my oldest friends, Fran Fusco, to bring the Debbie Ford trained eye, heart, and soul to bear and to make sure I had done her work justice. Fran introduced me to Debbie Ford, for which I am forever grateful. She made sure that this book could do what I wished: encourage its readers to study Debbie's work.

To further ensure Debbie's approval from beyond, I asked her sister, author and thought leader Arielle Ford, to look at the manuscript. She read it cover to cover, and then graciously endorsed it. This allowed Christine LeBlond at Red Wheel/Weiser to consider the manuscript seriously and decide that this was the breakup guide for which she had been waiting.

And, finally, the two most important men in my life. My dad instilled in me the thread of DNA that reads: "You can do this!" Even at the most excruciating moments on the road from inspiration to the book you hold in your hands,

I was spurred on by him. He is beaming with pride from beyond. If only he had been alive to meet the other most important man in my life—an angel, actually—Master John Douglas, who has always cheered me on with unconditional enthusiasm, while also continually clearing all that dims my Mighty Flame. Master John kept saying about this book just exactly what my dad would have said with the same beaming smile and heart: "It's going to be great!" He continues to remove more and more of what comes between me and my superhero, drawing me closer and closer to the Divine and reminding me always to see, hear, feel, and know love everywhere. I bow to him in body, mind, and spirit.

I am blessed beyond measure for the barn-raising level of support I received from all the superheroes mentioned here. Super Humility is mine and my deep gratitude is theirs.

Superhero Resources

Threads of all of these resources are woven throughout the book. I encourage you to explore the ones that resonate with you most.

Master John Douglas: If you want to clear your saboteurs, reveal your unconscious blocks, and open your heart even wider—if you want to help make this world a better place with your superhero heart—Master John Douglas is unlike anything else on the planet at this moment. He has many tools available to help you in your evolution. There is nothing among his offerings (events, teleseminars, products) that I would not recommend, but the MP3s that you can download from his website provide immediate superhero tools of unfathomable power. For instance, *Subconscious Repair* can be used on a weekly basis specifically to help with saboteurs.

Website: *masterangels.org*

Debbie Ford/The Ford Institute: If I met one of my primary goals with this book, you are now inspired to do more shadow work. Debbie Ford passed away in 2013, but her unique and powerful shadow work lives on through the coaches she trained. Fran Fusco (mentioned throughout this book) is a master coach who was trained by Debbie and then was hired to be an executive at the Ford Institute. She coaches privately now and the work is done over the phone so you can do your own deep shadow work from the comfort of your home.

Website: *thefordinstitute.com/franfusco*

Reverend Ed Bacon: Reverend Bacon is in the business of prying our hearts open a little wider so that we can feel God through love, feel love through God, and be even more powerful Superheroes of Love. His book *8 Habits of Love: Open Your Heart, Open Your Mind* gives practical everyday heart-opening tips for all of us, no matter what our faith.

Website: *8habitsoflove.com*

Marianne Williamson: Marianne introduced me to *A Course in Miracles* in the 1980s and it proved to be a beloved tool for me for many years. What a gift Marianne is to the world. I was shocked by how tiny she is when I met her, because I feel as if she holds all of our individual hearts as well as our collective heart. How does she do it?

She has a way of encouraging transformation and issuing prayers with both a surgical precision and a supremely gentle hand.

Website: *mariannewilliamson.com*

Mark Nepo: One of my favorite heart-softening tools is his book *The Book of Awakening: Having the Life You Want by Being Present to the Life You Have.* This book is one of the reasons I chose my publisher, as they published what I consider to be the daily bible that made a difference for me.

Website: *marknepo.com*

Rumi: *The Essential Rumi* by Coleman Barks is one of my favorites, but you can't go wrong with anything translated by Barks. As one friend said: "Coleman Barks doesn't just translate Rumi, he's a medium for him."

Arielle Ford: A perfect next step for those who wish to create a new relationship out of the clearing that this book has created. Arielle has a beat on helping people open their hearts to find their soul mates.

Website: *soulmatesecret.com*

Gay and Katie Hendricks: They make the dance of love look breathtakingly lovely and lyrical after thirty years together. All your superpowers can be honed under their tutelage.

Website: *heartsintrueharmony.com*

Don Miguel Ruiz: If you haven't read his book *The Four Agreements*, do. If you read it long ago, do it again. This book says it all and teaches the "Don't take *anything* personally" lesson like nothing else can.

Website: *miguelruiz.com*

Superhero Resources: Come on over to the Superhero of Love website, where we have live links to all kinds of resources that can help you strengthen your superpowers and stay awake and juiced up so you can fly, fly, fly!

Website: *superherooflove.com*

Superhero Thoughts

If you'd like to jot down your superhero thoughts or inspirations, here's a special sacred place just for that.

_____

_____

_____

_____

_____

_____

_____

_____

_____

_____

_____

_____

_____

_____

_____

_____

_____

_____

_____

_____

_____

_____

_____

_____

_____

_____

_____

_____

_____

_____

_____

_____

_____

_____

_____

_____

_____

_____

_____

_____

_____

_____

_____

_____

_____